Introduction to Sales Tax for Amazon FBA Sellers

Information and Tips to Help FBA Sellers
Understand Tax Law

Current as of July 1, 2012

Michael Rice & Kat Simpson

Kat Simpson Enterprises

2012

Complying with Sales Tax Laws as an Amazon Fulfillment seller

Rice, Michael & Simpson, Kat

Copyright © 2012 Kat Simpson Enterprises. All rights reserved.

EDITED BY: Jeff Simpson

FIRST PRINTING: July 2012

ISBN-13: **978-1477448403**

ISBN-10: **1477448403**

Printed in the United States of America

Foreword and cover art by Chris Green of ScanPower.com

Cover photo by istockphoto.com

When Michael and Kat asked if they should write a book about sales tax and Amazon, I said, "Absolutely!"

This is a subject that is not only confusing, but also constantly changing. Laws change, rules change, and just when you think you have it all figured out, something else changes. We're living a time where things change fast and technology is allowing us to do things that simply were not possible just a few, short years ago.

In many cases, the laws were written during a time when no one expected businesses to be conducting business the way that they are doing so today. The concept of 'nexus' still goes over the heads of many online sellers.

Because of these rapid changes, it's important to stay current on tax laws not only to keep your business out of hot water, but more importantly to keep the most money in your pocket!

I have known Michael and Kat for many years and it is a joy to work with people who authentically enjoy teaching and helping online sellers.

Due to the constantly changing nature of the subject matter presented in this book, I encourage all readers to check their website for the most up-to-date information as well as join and participate in their online discussion groups.

When I wrote my first book, *Retail Arbitrage*, everything was current and accurate at the time of printing. A few months later, things changed! New rules and new fee structures (among other things) were introduced. Such are the limitations of the written word when writing about topics that change so fast. Thankfully, we have the Internet to publish updates as well as writing revised and updated books.

I also recommend that everyone have their own CPA who is familiar with multi-state online businesses. Remember, if your CPA does not SAVE you more money than they cost you, FIRE THEM and find a better CPA!

I hope that you find this book as informative and useful as I have.

To your success,

Chris Green

Chris Green

ScanPower.com

Author of *Retail Arbitrage: The Blueprint for Buying Retail Products to Resell Online*

About the Authors:

Michael K. Rice, CMI

Managing Director

Michael is the Managing Director of Diligencia, LLC based in Houston, Texas. He advises and assists clients on various sales and use tax matters including; audit management/assistance business registrations/start up, compliance, transaction planning and refund reviews.

With more than 12 years of sales and use tax experience, Michael has spent time in both the public and private sector. Prior to forming Diligencia, LLC, Michael worked for a mid-cap oil and gas services and construction company managing all indirect taxes including sales/use, federal excise and property taxes. Prior to that Michael was with one of the largest independent power producers in the United States managing the sales/use tax function. In that role, Michael was also responsible for management and maintenance of the Sabrix tax engine as well as the integration of the tax engine with the company enterprise resource program PeopleSoft.

Michael also has public accounting / consulting experience, spending 4 years with Grant Thornton LLP serving clients from industries such as retail, manufacturing, oil and gas services, and telecommunications.

Additionally, Michael has served on the other side of the table as an auditor for the Louisiana Parishes performing sales and use tax audits of various industries from retail to manufacturing.

Michael's experience in multi-state sales and use taxation includes: providing sales/use tax compliance services, identifying and obtaining state tax refunds based on industry specific issues, managing and conducting state and local tax audits, assisting clients with voluntary disclosure agreements and private letter ruling requests, conducting FAS 5 provision reviews, researching and providing resolutions for a wide range of state tax issues, developing sales and use taxability matrices based on client and industry specific issues.

Michael is a member of the Institute for Professionals in Taxation and has obtained the CMI destination for professional recognition in the field of sales/use tax.

Education

Bachelors of Business Administration-Stephen F. Austin State University

Certification

Michael is a certified member of the Institute for Professionals in Taxation (CMI-s), which recognizes professional accomplishments in the field of sales, and use taxation.

About the Authors:

Kathy "Kat" Simpson

When Kathy "Kat" Simpson's husband became permanently disabled she knew she had to focus on her business to support her family and the Web and eBay was her choice of venues.

Kathy "Kat" Simpson is an established eCommerce expert and entrepreneur with online businesses since 1997. She is the owner of Kat's Boutique and successfully sells cross channel on several online platforms. Kat's Boutique can be found on eBay and Amazon.

Kat is a strong supporter of women entrepreneurs and donates 10% of her eBay sales to Mi Esperanza– The Women of My Hope. Kat is also the Chief Bling Officer for the annual breast cancer fundraiser, Bling My Bra, campaign founded by her friend Beth Cherkowsky.

Kat is a shooting star seller on eBay with over 15,000 feedback and has presented workshops at the Kansas Jubilee as well as being a featured speaker at the 2012 SCOE event in Seattle this September.

Kat has successfully co-hosted several ecommerce podcasts such as: eBay and Beyond; The River, The Ranch and the Bay, eCom Connections and is currently the host of FBA RADIO with Chris Green, Lisa Suttora & Bob Willey.

Kat keeps current with the ever-changing landscape of ecommerce and Social Networking as an eBay Education Specialist, a contributor to eBay Radio, the eBayInk Blog, a member of OSI Rockstars, Web Seller's Circle and she stays active on both Facebook and Twitter.

Kat is also very active in the lives of her 5 children and 3 grandchildren.

Legal Disclaimer –

While Michael Rice is a tax professional, the advice in this book is not to be taken as personal, specific tax advice. Each unique set of facts could give rise to different tax determinations discussed herein. Please consult a tax professional for specific tax guidance. This book is intended to be a general guide to signing up for and collecting sales tax for sellers on Amazon.com

To your success,

Michael Rice & Kat Simpson

Table of Contents

Chapter 1 – Introduction to Sales Taxation 1

Chapter 2 – Nexus 5

Chapter 3 – Registration with the Department of Revenue and Internal Revenue Service 11

Chapter 4 – Example Forms for Registration 19

Chapter 5 – Sales Tax Compliance 59

Chapter 6 – Resale Exemptions 67

Chapter 7 – Audit Issues 71

Chapter 8 – Setting Up Your Amazon Account For Sales Tax 75

Chapter 9 – Finding My Numbers...79

Chapter 10 – Conclusion..81

Chapter 1 – Introduction to Sales Taxation

Caveat: The information contained in this chapter should not be considered tax advice, but rather a guide from which you can inquire about fact-specific situations, which could lead to different answers based on the facts presented. Every State and some local taxing jurisdictions have specific sales/use tax statutes, rules and regulations, which govern the imposition of the relevant taxing jurisdictions sales/use tax law. In this chapter you will find use of the words "generally", "in general", "typically", "traditionally", "usually" or some variation thereof to describe the majority of sales/use rules and situations discussed below. Please consult a qualified sales tax professional for more specific answers to your situation

HISTORY and OVERVIEW:

The concept of taxing retail sales of tangible personal property has been around for quite some time. In 1930, Mississippi was the first state in the United States to impose a sales tax as we now know it. Since that time thousands of taxing jurisdictions (state and locals included) have imposed some form of taxation on retail sales of tangible personal property. On a state level, 45 states and the District of Columbia impose a general sales tax (Alaska, Delaware, Montana, New Hampshire and Oregon do not impose a state level sales/use tax). In general terms, all states that impose a sales tax also impose a use tax as a complementary tax to the sales tax with the general difference being that a sales tax is imposed at the time of sale of the tangible personal property and collected by the seller of the tangible personal property, whereas a use tax typically is imposed upon the purchaser or the consumer/user of the property.

Traditionally, the sales tax has been assessed on all sales of tangible personal property not specifically exempted (i.e., an exemption certificate is provided or the item category is excluded from the tax base). NOTE: sales tax is also assessed on services specifically enumerated as taxable under statute but in this chapter we are focused on sales of tangible personal property at retail. Typically any product you can sell online and ship to a customer would be considered tangible personal property, items such as books, clothing, toys, games, computer hardware and even computer software, just to name a few.

To properly understand retail sales tax we must examine each aspect of a retail sales transaction that is tangible personal property, retail sales and sales for resale.

Tangible personal property is generally defined as movable, corporeal property that is visible to our senses. Tangible and corporeal mean something that is discernible by touch. Tangible property is something that is visible, real or something with material or physical presence. This definition immediately excludes patents, copyrights, bonds, stocks, etc., which are intangibles.

Retail sale or sale at retail is generally defined as the sale of tangible personal property to all persons irrespective of the nature of their business including sales for resale and sales to the ultimate consumer or end user.

Sales for resale are generally exempt from sales and use tax because they are intermediate transactions that are sales to vendors, who in turn will charge sales tax upon their retail sale to the final or end user.

Without going into detail with regard to services, please note that in general, tangible personal property purchased with the intent to sell the item in its current form with no modifications is a resale transaction and generally exempt, whereas tangible personal property for use in a service may not qualify for resale exemption. In order to qualify for a resale exemption, a seller must possess a state issued tax identification number.

(More on sales tax identification numbers and resale certificates later in the book.)

Chapter 2 – Nexus

The information discussed below regarding Nexus specific to online retailers is current as of April 27, 2012. Current litigation and legislation combined with your specific fact pattern could change whether the nexus standard has been met.

Nexus is a term used in state and local taxation and refers to the connections, links or contacts (both quantitative and qualitative) between a political (taxing) jurisdiction and a taxpayer (business). If a taxpayer has sufficient nexus with a state, it will usually be deemed to be "doing business" in that state and liable for that states' taxes. In short, nexus determines whether or not a company is required to register and begin complying with a state's tax laws. It is further important to note that nexus varies by tax type. For sales tax nexus, generally all that is needed is a physical presence in the state. The physical presence can be created by employees, independent contractors, or the ownership (including inventory) or leasing of property in the state.

The topic of nexus for online sellers, especially those which could be considered affiliates of major online retailers, such as Amazon, has been an extremely hot topic in recent years. States have taken legal action against Amazon, Overstock, and Barnes and Noble Online, etc. and have increasingly pushed for more legislative action to resolve the question of affiliate nexus. I could personally write an entire book on the topic as it has been litigated time and time again with slightly different fact patterns and court rulings. To obtain my professional certification in sales taxation I was tested over 5 of the most important nexus related cases. I will not go over those in detail, but will discuss the one which comes up in the mainstream media and is the current standard by which nexus cases are generally decided, that is *Quill vs. North Dakota,* 504 U.S. (298) 1992. This US Supreme Court held in this case that a business must have a physical presence in a taxing jurisdiction in order for the taxing jurisdiction to require it to collect sales tax. However, the court explicitly stated that Congress can overrule that decision through legislation.

AMAZON and NEXUS:

At this point I feel the need to discuss Amazon's specific sales tax quandary (for lack of a better word) because they are currently the newsmaker on the topic of sales tax collections by online retailers and have the most pending litigation. In my opinion there are three aspects of Amazon's sales tax dilemma:

> 1. States which are attempting to force Amazon to collect via their own legislative actions (AKA "Amazon Laws")
> 2. States which are brokering deals with Amazon to build warehouses or fulfillment centers and create jobs in exchange for a delay in Amazon's obligation to collect their sales tax and
> 3. States in which Amazon clearly has nexus and is currently collecting the sales tax on retail sales.

Each of the above aspects has a subset of states (and even overlapping states) and actions of which I will mention the highlights in the discussions below.

Here is where the fun starts! Amazon currently collects tax on their retail sales in 5 states, Kansas, Kentucky, New York, North Dakota and Washington State. Yet this leaves the states of Arizona, Delaware, Indiana, Nevada, Pennsylvania, South Carolina, Tennessee and Virginia as states where Amazon or an affiliate company (entirely different argument there) has a fulfillment center.

Of the states in which a fulfillment center is located but Amazon does not currently collect tax, Arizona, Indiana, Nevada and South Carolina have essentially brokered (or are in the process of brokering) a deal with Amazon to begin collection of sales tax. The following states will begin to have their tax collected by Amazon on the date below (unless Congress acts sooner):

- California – September 2013
- Indiana – 2014 (presumably January)
- New Jersey – July 2013
- Nevada – 2014 (presumably January)
- South Carolina – date to be determined but currently proposed is a 5-year exemption, the longest exemption to date of the states to broker deals.
- Tennessee – 2014 (presumably January)
- Texas – July 1, 2012

Several states have attempted to pass their own "Amazon law" which would close the nexus loop hole in their state for online retailers and require Amazon and its affiliates to begin collecting tax on taxable retail sales in their state. Some of the states in this category are: Iowa, Minnesota, Mississippi, Missouri and New Jersey (which is stayed because of the deal Amazon made with the state).

You may have noticed from above that while *Quill vs. North Dakota* was a U.S. Supreme Court case, the court explicitly stated that Congress can overrule that decision through legislation. Currently there are three different bills which aim to do just that:

1. Main Street Fairness Act (S. 1452 / H.R. 2701)
2. Marketplace Equity Act (H.R. 3179)
3. Marketplace Fairness Act (S.1832)

Each of these bills appears to still be "alive," but they all serve to do similar functions - require out of state (remote) sellers to collect sales tax in states in which their customers were located without regard to nexus. These three bills would serve to change the way sales tax is collected and should be watched carefully. Although, if major developments happen with them you can be sure most of the major news media outlets would be reporting those developments.

Now, the question is:

How does this affect me, the online retailer, who is participating in Amazon's FBA program and currently with inventory in one of Amazon's fulfillment centers?

Well, the answer can be complicated, but I will give you the technical answer and best practice approach to staying compliant with the current nexus standard and various sales tax laws. If you currently maintain inventory in an Amazon fulfillment center in a state in which you do not reside or in which your business is not domiciled, then you probably still meet the nexus standard as defined under *Quill vs. North Dakota* and you should register your business in that state and begin collecting sales tax on taxable sales. Notice that I mentioned inventory in a state in which you do not reside or a state in which your business is not domiciled. Your business still owns the inventory and therefore your business has a physical presence in that state. There are arguments which center around how much inventory constitutes a minimum physical presence and the determination is on a state-by-state basis but generally, maintaining an inventory of tangible personal property for sale to end users or consumers will be enough to meet the threshold of nexus.

Chapter 3 – Registration with the Department of Revenue and Internal Revenue Service

REGISTRATIONS: Online vs. Paper

Before beginning the registration process, it is important to note that while most states do offer an online registration option, it is not required to be completed online. However, there are a few differences between the two:

1. The online application will skip certain sections based on your answers to required sections. With the paper application you must read carefully which sections you are required to fill out versus sections you can skip.
2. The online applications do not allow you to skip some questions for which you may not know the answer such as "other taxes for which you may be liable". A question you would probably ask your accountant.

LOCATION ADDRESS:

During the application process you will be asked for the address of your business. It is important to note that you are considered an "out of state seller" in states which are not your "home state" or state of residence. I recommend NOT using the address of the Amazon warehouse because while you might maintain inventory at that location, it is not your location. As such, where the application asks for a City, County, etc. of your location, you can use your home state address and leave sections such as County blank. The online application (as noted above) might default and require you to answer, but they should have a selection for the "out of state vendors".

OBTAINING A SALES TAX LICENSE:

In order to help you get started, should you choose to register with the DOR of the fulfillment center states, I wanted to provide a link to each state where there is a fulfillment center and the application for registration for a sales tax permit:

- Arizona - http://www.azdor.gov/
  - http://www.azdor.gov/Business/TransactionPrivilegeTax.aspx
  - Application-
    http://www.azdor.gov/LinkClick.aspx?fileticket=NhqcEr38FAA%3d&tabid=85

- Delaware – no state imposed sales tax

- Indiana - http://www.in.gov/dor/
  - http://www.in.gov/dor/3744.htm
  - Application - https://secure.in.gov/apps/dor/bt1/

- Kansas - http://www.ksrevenue.org/
  - http://www.ksrevenue.org/business.html
  - Application - http://www.ksrevenue.org/pdf/cr16.pdf
  - Or online here - https://www.kansas.gov/businesscenter/

- Kentucky - http://revenue.ky.gov/
  - http://revenue.ky.gov/business/register.htm
  - Application - http://revenue.ky.gov/NR/rdonlyres/4A9BEB16-844E-4F8B-B095-8825257E54B5/0/10A1001011.pdf
  - Or online here - https://secure.kentucky.gov/sos/ftbr/welcome.aspx

- Nevada - http://tax.state.nv.us/
  - http://tax.state.nv.us/About%20taxes%20and%20Faqs.html#Registering_with_the_department
  - Application - http://tax.state.nv.us/documents/app01b.pdf
  - Or online here - https://www.nevadatax.nv.gov/web/

- Pennsylvania
  - http://www.revenue.state.pa.us/portal/server.pt/community/revenue_home/10648
  - http://www.revenue.state.pa.us/portal/server.pt/community/businesses/11406
  - Online application here -
  - http://www.doreservices.state.pa.us/BusinessTax/PA100/FormatSelection.htm

- South Carolina - http://www.sctax.org/default.htm
  - https://www.scbos.sc.gov/
  - Online application here –
  - https://www.scbos.sc.gov/Start_Your_Business/Registering_for_the_First_Time.aspx

- Tennessee - http://www.state.tn.us/revenue/
  - http://www.state.tn.us/revenue/tntaxes/salesanduse.shtml
  - Application -

- http://www.state.tn.us/revenue/forms/general/f13005_1.pdf
- Instructions -
- http://www.state.tn.us/revenue/forms/general/applinst.pdf
- Online: https://apps.tn.gov/bizreg/index.html

- Virginia - http://www.tax.virginia.gov/
  - http://www.tax.virginia.gov/site.cfm?alias=BusinessHome
  - http://www.tax.virginia.gov/site.cfm?alias=RegBus
  - Online application –
  - https://www.ireg.tax.virginia.gov/VTOL/Login.seam
  - Paper application –
  - http://www.tax.virginia.gov/taxforms/Business/Business%20Registration/R-1.pdf

- Washington - http://dor.wa.gov/Content/Home/Default.aspx
  - http://bls.dor.wa.gov/
  - Online - http://bls.dor.wa.gov/taxregistration.aspx
  - Paper - http://bls.dor.wa.gov/forms/700028.pdf

What to expect when you are expecting a sales tax license:

Once you have navigated the cumbersome but not overly complicated state sales tax license application you might be wondering if your obligation to collect tax has begun? The technical answer is yes. Once you start selling taxable items in a state in which you have nexus you should collect sales tax on those sales. The difficulty, however, is that the mechanism to allow you to collect sales tax is more than likely utilizing Amazon's tax collection service. Problem; Amazon requires you to submit your state issued tax identification number (NOT your FEIN) to them so all involved can rest assured you are properly licensed to collect AND remit the applicable states sales tax. If this is a significant or material amount, I recommend you discuss options with your tax accountant.

Depending upon your chosen application method (paper or online), it could take as much as four weeks to receive a response back with your approved paperwork and license. Some states are much faster than others, for various reasons. There is no reason to become alarmed if you have not received anything back, but if you feel the need to touch base with the state department of revenue that is fine as well. Typically on the "contact us" page of the department of revenue there will be a phone number. You can call and ask to speak to the "sales tax licensing" or "business registration" division and you will be connected. Have your FEIN handy, as this will be required for the state representative to look up your application status.

Uh-oh, there was a problem with your application, now what? This is not a huge problem and actually happens quite often that a "required field" was unintentionally left blank, or you missed the notice that an application fee is required, or in the case of California, you neglected to send in a copy of your driver's license (yes, the California Board of Equalization will hold up your application pending receipt of a copy of your driver's license).

The state will typically do one of three things:

1. Return mail your application with a letter indicating the missing information and directing you to complete said missing information and return it for finalization.
2. Call you at the contact telephone number (important to give this) you provided and ask for the information over the phone. This speeds up the process immensely and is typically used if the missing information is a left off required field as opposed to missing supporting documentation such as copies of driver's licenses.
3. Send you an email (also important to provide) stating your application is missing information and to contact the department of revenue at your earliest convenience.

After providing any missing information, you will receive your hot off the press, freshly minted, "new in box", sales tax license (some states refer to it as a permit, same thing). I recommend keeping a copy of everything, and when I say everything, I mean copies of all written correspondence between you, your company and the state, copies of applications sent in and originals of what the state sends back to you in the form of licenses, certificates, etc. I also recommend documenting telephone calls between you and the state department of revenue. At this point I would suggest using your best judgment on when to document a call, but anytime you RECEIVE a call from the state, I suggest documenting.

The relevant items to note when documenting a call are:

1. Date and Time of Call
2. Topic of the Conversation
3. Who you spoke with. Full name (if they are willing to provide) but at least a name and representative number or last initial.
4. Department in which the representative works (*e.g.*, Audit, Compliance, Registration, etc)
5. Relevant details of the call such as if the representative asks you to provide additional documentation, etc.
6. Solution discussed. If the representative mentions the problem will be cleared up if you perform A, B and C then note what you need to do and follow through.

Waiting on the state is not necessarily a bad thing. It does, however, take a little patience and typically the state will return the same level of patience and provide assistance for newly formed businesses that are trying to comply with the law.

Chapter 4 – Example Forms for Registration

In this chapter we will include some of the forms you will see when you go to the download sites listed in chapter three. We felt there was no need to include all of every form. Most will ask the same questions in different ways and all are many pages long. Some states include the instructions with the form you download; while some separate them and you will have two files to download. One the instructions and the other the actual form. Many of the forms can be submitted over the internet, others will have to be downloaded, filled in and then either faxed or mailed via the USPS to the different state addresses you will find in the instructions.

ARIZONA – The online application is slightly different than this example but all the information they ask for is the same with the exception of asking you what County you are registering for. The Amazon Arizona warehouse is in Goodyear, Arizona, which is Maricopa County. Arizona will charge you $15 for the county and $2 for the city of Goodyear. They are not set up to accept payment online for the application so you will have to mail in the signature page of the application with your check for $17.

INDIANA – You are able to finish the application and pay the $25 fee online for Indiana. You will have to have a Federal Employee

Identification Number (FEIN) to file this application and if you file as a Sole Proprietor they also require your Social Security Number. There is an extra $1.52 added if you use their convenience feature and pay online so the total charged will be $26.52.

KANSAS – I actually found the online Kansas site too difficult to navigate. I kept getting into a circle of links that wanted me to register my business in KS even though the site told me it was not necessary to register in order to get a tax license. So I printed out the forms faxed them in. There was no charge.

KENTUCKY – Kentucky has a great setup. You can do the complete application online and there is no charge at all. Kentucky does require you to sign up with a user name and password for the site.

NEVADA - To use the online registration form for Nevada you must use the latest Internet Explorer browser. Nevada's registration form requires both an EIN and a Social Security Number. The registration fee is $15 plus whatever 'Security Deposit' they place on your account. This seems to be based on what sales you estimate. I estimated $10,000 per month with $10 per month in Nevada and my deposit was $0 (Kat). You must use your bank account to pay on this site as they do not accept credit cards.

PENNSYLVANIA – Very easy to use site but must be accessed with Internet Explorer. Fee is $0 and all information can be submitted electronically.

SOUTH CAROLINA – Very easy to use site but also the most expensive. $50 fee.

TENNESSEE – Very easy – use Internet Explorer browser to avoid errors. No Fee.

VIRGINIA – The second one I had to fax in. No cost

WASHINGTON – Not hard to use. $20

Total cost $128.52

JT-1UC-001 (7/11)

ARIZONA JOINT TAX APPLICATION

IMPORTANT: *Incomplete applications WILL NOT BE PROCESSED. All required information is designated with asterisk* *
To complete this application see attached Instructions. Please return Complete application with appropriate license fee(s) to: **License & Registration Section, Department of Revenue, PO BOX 29032, Phoenix AZ 85038-9032.**

To complete this online, go to   www.aztaxes.gov

Section A: Taxpayer Information (Print legibly or type the information on this application.)		

1. License Type (Check all that apply) *
- [X] Transaction Privilege Tax (TPT)
- [ ] Withholding/Unemployment Tax (if hiring employees)
- [ ] Use Tax
- [ ] TPT For Cities ONLY

2. Type of Ownership *   *Use your own structure*
- [ ] Individual / Sole Proprietorship
- [ ] Partnership
- [ ] Professional Limited Liability
- [X] Limited Liability Company
- [ ] Limited Liability Partnership
- [ ] Corporation
  - State of Inc. _____
  - Date of Inc. _____
- [ ] Sub-Chapter S Corporation
- [ ] Association
- [ ] Trust
- [ ] Government
- [ ] Estate
- [ ] Joint Venture
- [ ] Receivership

Tax exempt organizations must attach a copy of the Internal Revenue Service letter of determination.

3. Federal Employer Identification Number (Required for Employers and Entities other than Sole Proprietors) or Social Security Number *
12-3456789   *must have*

4. Legal Business Name / Owner / Employing Unit *   *Name which is registered with your SOS office*
ABC Toys, LLC

5. Business or "Doing Business As" Name *	6. Business Phone Number *	7. Fax Number
ABC Toys	(555) 123-1212	

8. Mailing Address (Street, City, State, ZIP code) * *does not have to be in same state as registering*	9. Country
123 Main Street, Houston, Texas 77027	

10. Email Address	11. Is your business located on an Indian Reservation?
name@youremail.com	[ ] Yes If yes, _____ (See Section G for listing of Reservations) [X] No

12. Physical Location of Business (Street, City, State, ZIP code) Do not use PO Box or Route No. *	13. County
123 Main Street, Houston, Texas 77027	

For additional business locations, complete Section B-12

14. Are you a construction contractor? *	15. Did you acquire, or change the legal form of business of, all or part of an existing business? *
[ ] Yes (See Bonding Requirements below) [X] No	[ ] Yes If yes, you must complete the Unemployment Tax Information (Section D) [X] No

Bonding Requirements: Prior to the issuance of a Transaction Privilege Tax license, new or out-of-state contractors are required to post a Taxpayer Bond for Contractors, unless the Contractor qualifies for an exemption from the bonding requirement. The primary type of contracting being performed determines the amount of bond to be posted. Bonds may also be required from applicants who are delinquent in paying Arizona taxes or have a history of delinquencies. For more information on bonding, please see the "Taxpayer Bonds" publication, which is available online or at the Department of Revenue offices.

16. Description of Business (Must include type of merchandise sold or taxable activity; for employers, the type of employment) *
Retail seller of toys, books, games etc. to end users via on-line transactions

17. NAICS Code: (Select at least one Go to www.aztaxes.gov for a listing of codes) *
12345

18. Identification of Owner, Partners, Corporate Officers, Members / Managing Members or Officials of this employing unit

A. Name (Last, First, MI) *	B. Soc. Sec. No. *	C. Title *	D. % Owned *	E. Complete Residence Address *	F. Phone Number *
Your, Name	123-45-6789	Owner	100	123 Main Street, Houston, T	(555) 123-1212

If the owner, partners, corporate officers or combination of partners or corporate officers, members and/or managing members own more than 50% of or control another business in Arizona, attach a list of the businesses, percentages owned and unemployment insurance account numbers.

ADOR 10194 (7/11)

Arizona – continued.

Section B: Transaction Privilege Tax (TPT)

1. Date Business Started in Arizona *	2. Date Sales Began *	3. What is your anticipated annual income for your first twelve months of business?
04/01/2012	04/15/2012	

4. Business Classes (Select at least one. See Section H for a listing of business classes on page 4) *

   Retail - 017

5. TPT Filing Method	6. Does your business sell tobacco products?	7. Does your business sell new motor vehicle tires or vehicles?
☒ Cash Receipts	☐ Yes If yes, ☐ Retailer OR	☒ No
☐ Accrual	☒ No ☐ Distributor	☐ Yes (You will be required to file a TR-1.)

8. Are you a seasonal filer?	If yes, please check the months in which you intend to do business:
☐ Yes ☒ No	Jan Feb Mar Apr May Jun Jul Aug Sep Oct Nov Dec

9. Location of Tax Records (Street Address, City, State and ZIP code) Do not use PO Box or Route No. *

   Your office or home office, where you keep your records

10. Name of Company or Person to Contact	11. Phone Number
Your Name	

For additional locations, complete the following: (If more space is needed, please attach additional sheets)

12. "Doing Business As" Name for this Location	13. Phone Number

14. Physical Location Address (Do not use PO Box or Route No.)		
15. City	17. State	18. ZIP code

typically you will not need these sections

19. "Doing Business As" Name for this Location	20. Phone Number

21. Physical Location Address (Do not use PO Box or Route No.)

22. City	23. County	24. State	25. ZIP code

Section C: Program Cities / License Fees Below is a list of cities and towns licensed by the Arizona Department of Revenue.

City/Town	Code	Fee	No. of Loc	Total	City/Town	Code	Fee	No. of Loc	Total	City/Town	Code	Fee	No. of Loc	Total
Benson	BS	5.00			Hayden	HY	5.00			Show Low	SL	2.00		
Bisbee	BB	1.00			Holbrook	HB	1.00			Sierra Vista	SR	1.00		
Buckeye	BE	2.00			Huachuca City	HC	2.00			Snowflake	SN	2.00		
Camp Verde	CE	2.00			Jerome	JO	2.00			South Tucson	ST	2.00		
Carefree	CA	10.00			Kearny	KN	2.00			Springerville	SV	5.00		
Casa Grande	CG	2.00			Kingman					St. Johns	SJ	2.00		
Cave Creek	CK	20.00			Lake Hav					Star Valley	SY	2.00		
Chino Valley	CV	2.00			Litchfield					Superior	SI	2.00		
Clarkdale	CD	2.00			Mammoth					Surprise	SP	10.00		
Clifton	CF	2.00			Marana					Taylor	TL	2.00		
Colorado City	CC	2.00			Maricopa					Thatcher	TC	2.00		
Coolidge	CL	2.00			Miami					Tolleson	TN	2.00		
Cottonwood	CW	2.00			Oro Valley					Tombstone	T5	1.00		
Dewey/Humboldt	DH	2.00			Page					Tusayan	TY	2.00		
Duncan	DC	2.00			Paradise					Wellton	WT	2.00		
Eagar	EG	10.00			Parker					Wickenburg	WB	2.00		
El Mirage	EM	15.00			Patagonia					Williams	WL	2.00		
Eloy	EL	10.00			Payson	PS	2.00			Winkelman	WM	2.00		
Florence	FL	2.00			Pima	PM	2.00			Winslow	WS	10.00		
Fountain Hills	FH	2.00			Pinetop/Lakeside	PP	2.00			Youngtown	YT	10.00		
Fredonia	FD	10.00			Prescott Valley	PL	2.00			Yuma	YM	2.00		
Gila Bend	GI	2.00			Quartzsite	QZ	2.00							
Gilbert	GB	2.00			Queen Creek	QC	2.00							
Globe	GL	2.00			Safford	SF	2.00							
Goodyear	GY	5.00			Sahuarita	SA	5.00							
Guadalupe	GU	2.00			San Luis	SU	2.00							

As an online seller you will typically not need this in Arizona, if the state requires it upon your application you would select the city where Amazon has a warehouse

▶ **Please Note:** City fees are subject to change (go to our website for updates). For cities not listed above, please contact the cities directly. Your license will not be issued until all fees are paid.	Total of City Fees:
	State Fees $12.00 X _____ Number of Locations:
	TOTAL Fees:

ADOR 10194 (7/11)

Arizona – continued.

Section D: Withholding/Unemployment Tax Information

1. Date Employees First Hired in Arizona. * **None-Out of State**	2. Are you liable for Federal Unemployment Tax? ☐ Yes If yes, what was the first year of liability? ☐ No Year _____	3. Are individuals performing services that are excluded from withholding or unemployment tax? ☐ Yes If yes, describe the services: ☐ No

4. Do you have an IRS Ruling that grants an exclusion from Federal Unemployment Tax? ☐ Yes If yes, attach a copy of the Ruling Letter. ☐ No	5. Do you have or have you previously had an Arizona Unemployment Tax Number? ☐ No ☐ Yes If yes, Business Name _____ Unemployment Number _____

6. Record of Arizona wages paid by calendar quarter for current and preceding calendar year.

YEAR	1ST QUARTER	2ND QUARTER	3RD QUARTER	4TH QUARTER

7. Weekly record of number of persons performing services in Arizona for current and preceding calendar year.

YEAR	JANUARY	FEBRUARY	MARCH	APRIL	MAY	JUNE

YEAR	JULY	AUGUST	SEPTEMBER	OCTOBER	NOVEMBER	DECEMBER

Complete this section if you acquired, or changed the legal form of business of, all or part of an existing Arizona business.

8. Date Acquired or Date Legal Form of Business changed *	9. Acquired, or Changed Legal Form of Business of, * ☐ All ☐ Part If part, to obtain an unemployment tax rate based on the business's previous account you must request it no later than 180 days after the date entered in item 8 of this section. See instructions.	10. Acquired by * ☐ Purchase ☐ Lease ☐ Other	If other, including change in legal form of business, explain:

Previous Owner Information or Previous Legal Form of Business Information (See instructions.)

11. Name(s) of Previous Owner(s) *	12. Business Name of Previous Owner(s) *

13. Current Mailing Address of Previous Owner(s) (Street, City, State, ZIP code)

14. Current Telephone Number of Previous Owner(s)	15. Unemployment Account Number of Previous Owner(s)

Voluntary Election of Unemployment Insurance Coverage (subject to Unemployment Tax Office approval).

16. The applicant, on behalf of the employing unit, voluntarily elects beginning January 1 of the current calendar year or the date employment started, if later, and continuing for not less than two calendar years, to:

☐ A. Be deemed an employer subject to Title 23, Chapter 4, Arizona Revised Statutes, to the same extent as all other such employers and provide unemployment insurance coverage to my workers performing services defined by law as employment, even though I have not met conditions requiring me to provide such coverage.

☐ B. Extend unemployment insurance coverage to workers referred to in item 2, above, by having the services they perform be deemed to constitute Employment by an employer subject to Title 23, Chapter 4, A.R.S.

Arizona – continued.

Section E: AZTaxes.gov Security Administrator (Authorized User)

By electing to register for www.aztaxes.gov you can have online access to account information, and file and pay Arizona transaction, use, and withholding taxes. You also designate authorized users to access these services.

☐ I Elect to Register to use aztaxes.gov to file and pay online. ←   **Your choice, online is faster**

☐ I DO NOT Elect to Register to use aztaxes.gov to file and pay online.

1. Authorized Users Last Name	2. Authorized Users First Name
3. Authorized Users Title	4. Authorized Users Social Security Number
5. Authorized Users Email Address	6. Authorized Users Phone Number

Section F: Signature(s) by individuals legally responsible for the business (required)

This application must be signed by either a sole owner, partners, corporate officer, managing member, the trustee, receiver or personal representative of an estate.

Under penalty of perjury I (we), the applicant, declare that the information provided on this application is true and correct. I (we) hereby authorize the security administrator, if one is listed in Section E, to access the AZTaxes.gov site for the business identified in Section A. This authority is to remain in full force and effect until the Arizona Department of Revenue has received written termination notification from an authorized officer.

Type or Print Name	Title	Signature	Date
Type or Print Name	Title	Signature	Date

THIS APPLICATION MUST BE COMPLETED, SIGNED AND RETURNED AS PROVIDED BY ARS § 23-722
Equal Opportunity Employer/Program • This document available in alternative formats by contacting the UI Tax Office.

Section G: Indian Reservation Codes

Indian Reservation (County)	Code	Indian Reservation (County)	Code	Indian Reservation (County)	Code	Indian Reservation (County)	Code
Ak-Chin (Pinal)	PNA	Hopi (Coconino)	COJ	Pascua-Yaqui (Maricopa)	MAN	Tohono O'dham (Pinal)	PNT
Cocopah (Yuma)	YMB	Hopi (Navajo)	NAJ	Pascua-Yaqui (Pima)	PMN	Tonto Apache (Gila)	GLU
Colorado River (La Paz)	LAC	Hualapai (Coconino)	COK	Salt River Pima-Maricopa (Mar.)	MAO	White Mtn Apache (Apache)	APD
Fort McDowell-Yavapai (Mar.)	MAE	Hualapai (Mohave)	MOK	San Carlos Apache (Gila)	GLP	White Mtn Apache (Gila)	GLD
Fort Mohave (Mohave)	MOF	Kaibab-Paiute (Coconino)	COL	San Carlos Apache (Graham)	GRP	White Mtn Apache (Graham)	GRD
Fort Yuma-Quechan (Yuma)	YMG	Kaibab-Paiute (Mohave)	MOL	San Carlos Apache (Pinal)	PNP	White Mtn Apache (Navajo)	NAD
Gila River (Maricopa)	MAH	Navajo (Apache)	APM	San Juan Southern Paiute (Coco.)	COQ	Yavapai Apache (Yavapai)	YAW
Gila River (Pinal)	PNH	Navajo (Coconino)	COM	Tohono O'Odham (Maricopa)	MAT	Yavapai Prescott (Yavapai)	YAX
Havasupai (Coconino)	COI	Navajo (Navajo)	NAM	Tohono O'Odham (Pima)	PMT		

Section H: Business Classes

Business Class	Code	Business Class	Code	Business Class	Code	Business Class	Code
Mining - Nonmetal	002	Commercial Lease	013	Use Tax - Utilities	026	Jet Fuel Tax	049
Utilities	004	Personal Property Rental	014	Rental Occupancy Tax	028	Jet Fuel Use Tax	051
Communications	005	Contracting - Prime	015	Use Tax Purchases	029	Rental Car Surcharge	053/055
Transporting	006	Retail	017	Use Tax from Inventory	030	Jet Fuel Tax > 10 million gallons	056
Private Car - Pipeline	007/008	Severance - Metalliferous Mining	019	Telecommunications Devices	033	Use Tax Direct Payments	129
Publication	009	Severance - Timbering Ponderosa	021	911 Wireless Telecommunications	036	911 Wireline Telecommunications	131
Job Printing	010	Severance - Timbering Other	022	Contracting - Owner Builder	037	Rental Car Surcharge - Stadium	153
Restaurants and Bars	011	Recreational Vehicle Surcharge	023	Municipal Water	041		
Amusement	012	Transient Lodging	025	Membership Camping	047		

Indiana Department of Revenue
Online Business Tax Application (BT-1)
Quick Start Guide

Welcome to the Indiana Department of Revenue online Business Tax Application (BT-1).

The online BT-1 is used to register a new or existing business for sales tax, withholding tax, out-of-state use tax, food and beverage tax, county innkeeper's tax, motor vehicle rental excise tax, prepaid sales tax on gasoline, or a combination of any of these taxes.

The online BT-1 is also used to add a location to an existing business account.

The online BT-1 is secure, easy to complete, and reduces the time it takes to register with the Indiana Department of Revenue. This quick start guide covers the basic steps for completing your application.

Step 1:   Review the **BT-1 checklist** for an overview of the information needed to complete the online application.

Step 2: Go   to https://secure.in.gov/apps/dor/bt1/ to begin the online process.

Step 3: Select   **start new** to begin a new business application.

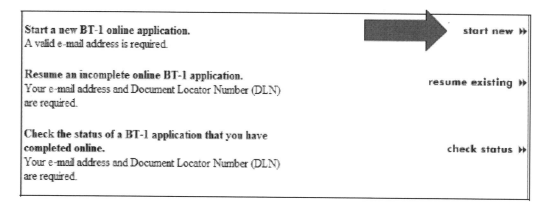

Start a new BT-1 online application.
A valid e-mail address is required.

start new ▸▸

Resume an incomplete online BT-1 application.
Your e-mail address and Document Locator Number (DLN) are required.

resume existing ▸▸

Check the status of a BT-1 application that you have completed online.
Your e-mail address and Document Locator Number (DLN) are required.

check status ▸▸

Indiana – continued.

Step 4: Enter the **Email Address** you wish to use for your contact with the Department during the application process and click **continue**.

If you are starting a new application, please enter your email address. An email will be sent to you with your Document Locator Number and instructions on how to resume your application if you leave the application.
Email Address: [   ]
continue ▶▶

Step 5: Select the appropriate **reason for filing the application** and click **continue**.

Please select the reason for filing this application :
You should select this since you are a new business in this state. ——→ ○ Starting a New Business
○ To Add a Location To an Existing Taxpayer ID
○ To Register Other Types to an Existing Location
continue ▶▶

Step 6: Enter the **Federal ID Number (FID/EIN)**, **Entity Name** or **Sole Owner Name**, and click **continue**. Note: The taxpayer identification number (TID) will also be requested if you are registering an existing business for a new tax type or adding a location to an existing account.

Please enter the following information :
Federal ID Number (FID/EIN): [   ]
Enter a *Sole Owner Name* if your organization type is *Sole Proprietor*. Otherwise, enter your *Entity Name*.
Legal Name, Partnership Name, Corporate Name, or Other Entity Name: [   ]
or Sole Owner Name: (first name, middle initial, last name, suffix) [   ] [ ] [   ] [ ]
To obtain a Federal ID Number (FID/EIN) if you do not have one, go to the IRS website
If you do not have a valid FEIN you will not be able to proceed with the registration ——→
continue ▶▶

Indiana – continued.

Step 7: Enter the **Business Contact Information** and click continue. **Important Note:** The **Document Locator Number (DLN)** will be displayed at the bottom of this screen. Please write this number down. You will need it for future reference.

Please enter the following Business Contact Information :

Contact Name:	
Daytime Phone Number:	ext.:
###-###-####	

continue ▶▶

Your Document Locator Number is: 10x000000028 . Please write this number down. (More Info)

Next Steps:

- Enter the requested information on the remaining screens to complete the online BT-1 application.

- Review the application to ensure it is correct prior to submitting it electronically to the Indiana Department of Revenue. A copy of the application can be printed after it has been submitted.

- The Indiana Department of Revenue will send you an email, with the status of your application, 48-72 hours after submission. If the application has successfully been submitted, you will receive your taxpayer identification number (TID). If there are any outstanding issues with the application, you will be asked to contact the Department.

- Please do not register for INtax until you have received official confirmation stating your application was successfully submitted to the Indiana Department of Revenue.

- Where applicable, Registered Retail Merchant Certificates will be mailed out 48-72 hours after successful submission of the BT-1 to the Indiana Department of Revenue.

- If you need additional assistance, please call the Indiana Department of Revenue at 317-233-4015. Be sure to have your Document Locator Number available when calling the Department.

Thank you for registering your business with the Indiana Department of Revenue using the online BT-1 Business Tax Application.

KANSAS BUSINESS TAX APPLICATION

PART 1 – REASON FOR APPLICATION (check one):

☐ New Business   ☐ Registration of Additional Tax Type(s)

Note: If registered but adding another business location, you need only complete Schedule CR-17 (page 13).

PART 2 – TAX TYPE (check the box for each tax type or license requested and complete the required Parts of this application):

☐ **Retailers' Sales Tax** ← place "X" in box
(Complete Parts 1, 2, 3, 4, 5 & 12)

☐ **Retailers' Compensating Use Tax**
(Complete Parts 1, 2, 3, 4, 5 & 12)

☐ **Consumers' Compensating Use Tax**
(Complete Parts 1, 2, 3, 4, 5 & 12)

☐ **Withholding Tax**
(Complete Parts 1, 2, 3, 4, 6 & 12)

☐ **Transient Guest Tax**
(Complete Parts 1, 2, 3, 4, 5 & 12)

☐ **Tire Excise Tax**
(Complete Parts 1, 2, 3, 4, 5 & 12)

☐ **Vehicle Rental Excise Tax**
(Complete Parts 1, 2, 3, 4, 5 & 12)

☐ **Dry**
(Complete Parts 1, 2, 3, 4, 5 & 12)

☐ **Liquor Enforcement Tax**
(Complete Parts 1, 2, 3, 4, 8 & 12)

☐ **Liquor Drink Tax**
(Complete Parts 1, 2, 3, 4, 9 & 12)

☐ **Cigarette Vending Machine Permit**
(Complete Parts 1, 2, 3, 4, 5, 10 & 12)

☐ **Retail Cigarette License**
(Complete Parts 1, 2, 3, 4, 5, 10 & 12)

☐ **Corporate Income Tax**
(Complete Parts 1, 2, 3, 4, 7 & 12)

☐ **Privilege Tax**
(Complete Parts 1, 2, 3, 4, 7 & 12)

☐ **Nonresident Contractor**
(Complete Parts 1, 2, 3, 4, 5, 11 & 12)

☐ **Water Protection / Clean Drinking Water Fee**
(Complete Parts 1, 2, 3, 4, 5 & 12)

> **IMPORTANT:** Effective July 1, 2010, businesses are required to **submit** Retailers' Sales, Compensating Use, and Withholding Tax returns **electronically.** See the electronic file and pay options available to you on page 8 or visit webtax.org.

PART 3 – BUSINESS INFORMATION (please type or print):

1. Type of Ownership (check one):   ☐ Sole Proprietor   ☐ Limited Partnership   ☐ General Partnership
   ☐ Limited Liability Partnership   ☐ Limited Liability Company   ☐ Federal Government   ☐ Other Government
   ☐ Non-Profit Corporation   ☐ Other _____ ⟶ Legal name
   ☐ S Corporation   Date of Incorporation: Month ____ Day ____ Year ____   State of Incorporation _____
   ☐ C Corporation   Date of Incorporation: Month ____ Day ____ Year ____   State of Incorporation _____

2. Business Name: ABC Toys, LLC   ⟵ does not have to be in Kansas

3. Business Mailing Address: 123 Main Street
   (Street, Route or PO Box - include apartment, suite, or lot number)
   Houston   Harris   Texas   77027
   (City)   *(County)*   *(State)*   *(Zip Code)*

4. Business Phone: (___) _____   Business Fax: (___) _____   Email: _____

5. Business Contact Person: _____   Phone: (___) _____

6. Federal Employer Identification Number (EIN): ___ ___ - ___ ___ ___ ___ ___ ___   (DO NOT en most small businesses are

7. Accounting Method (check one):   ☐ Cash Basis   ☐ Accrual Basis ⟵ cash basis

8. Describe your primary (taxable) business activity: online retail sales to end users
   Enter business classification NAICS Code (from Pub. KS-1500; see instructions): _____

9. Parent Company Name (if applicable): _____
   Parent Company EIN: ___ ___ - ___ ___ ___ ___ ___ ___
   Parent Company Address: _____
   (Street, Route or PO Box - include apartment, suite, or lot number)
   _____
   (City)   *(County)*   *(State)*   *(Zip Code)*

10. Subsidiaries (if applicable): *If more than two, please enclose a separate sheet.*
    Name: _____   EIN: ___ ___ - ___ ___ ___ ___ ___ ___
    Company Address: _____
    (Street, Route or PO Box - include apartment, suite, or lot number)
    _____
    (City)   *(County)*   *(State)*   *(Zip Code)*
    Name: _____   EIN: ___ ___ - ___ ___ ___ ___ ___ ___
    Company Address: _____
    (Street, Route or PO Box - include apartment, suite, or lot number)
    _____
    (City)   *(County)*   *(State)*   *(Zip Code)*

11. Have you or any member of your firm previously held a Kansas tax registration number?   ☐ No   ☐ Yes   If yes, list previous number or name of business: _____

Please visit e-ComSalesTax.com for more information

Kansas – continued.

ENTER YOUR EIN: ___ ___ - ___ ___ ___ ___ ___ ___ ___   **OR**   SSN: ___ ___ ___ - ___ ___ - ___ ___ ___ ___

PART 3 (continued)

12. List all Kansas registration numbers currently in use: _____ ← *more than likely answer is "N/A"*

13. List all registration numbers that need to be closed due to the filing of this application _____ *Answer is probably no for everyone, this indicates an entirely different set of rules, etc*

14. Are you registered with Streamlined Sales Tax (SST)? ☐ No ☐ Yes If yes, enter your _____

PART 4 – LOCATION INFORMATION (If you have only one business location, complete Part 4. If you have more than one business location, complete Part 4 and Form CR-17, page 13, for each additional location.)

1. Trade Name of Business: ABC Toys

2. Business Location: _____ ← *your mailing or office address* _____
   (Street address - Do not list PO Box)

   _____
   (City)   (County)   (State)   (Zip Code)

3. Is the business location within the city limits? ☐ No ☐ Yes If yes, what city? _____ *Typically no, you are an out of state seller*

4. Describe your primary business activity: _____
   Enter business classification NAICS Code (if known): _____

5. Business telephone number: ( ) _____

6. Is your business engaged in renting or leasing motor vehicles? ☐ No ☐ Yes Are the leases for more than 28 days? ☐ No ☐ Yes

7. Is this location a hotel, motel, or bed and breakfast? ☐ No ☐ Yes If yes, number of sleeping rooms available for rent/lease: _____

8. Do you sell new tires and/or vehicles with new tires? ☐ No ☐ Yes Estimate your monthly tire tax ($.25 per tire): $_____

9. If you are a dry cleaner or laundry retailer, do you have satellite locations or agents in businesses not classified as a dry cleaning or laundry facility? ☐ No ☐ Yes If yes, enclose additional page listing name, business type, address, city, state and zip code of each satellite location.

10. Are you a public water supplier making retail sales of water delivered through mains, lines, or pipes? ☐ No ☐ Yes

11. Do you make retail sales of motor vehicle fuels or special fuels? ☐ No ☐ Yes If yes, you must also have a Kansas Motor Fuel Retailers License. Complete and submit an application (MF-53) for each retail location.

PART 5 – SALES/COMPENSATING USE TAX

1. Date retail sales/compensating use began (or will begin) in Kansas under this ownership: _____ / _____ / _____

2. Do you operate more than one business location in Kansas? ☐ No ☐ Yes If yes, how many? _____ (Complete a Form CR-17 for each location in addition to the one listed in Part 4. Sales for all locations are reported on one return.)

3. Will sales be made from various temporary locations? ☐ No ☐ Yes

4. Do you ship or deliver merchandise to Kansas customers? ☐ No ☐ Yes

5. Do you purchase merchandise, equipment, fixtures and other items outside Kansas for your own use (not for resale) in Kansas on which you are not charged a sales tax? ☐ No ☐ Yes

6. Estimate your annual Kansas sales or compensating use tax liability:
   ☐ $80 & under (annual filer)   ☐ $81 - $3,200 (quarterly filer)   ☐ $3,201 - $32,000 (monthly filer)   ☐ $32,001 - $45,000 (Pre-paid monthly filer)

7. If your business is seasonal, list the months you operate: _____

8. Are you performing labor services in connection with the construction, reconstruction, or repair of commercial buildings or facilities?
   ☐ No ☐ Yes

9. Do you sell natural gas, electricity, or heat (propane gas, LP gas, coal, wood) to residential or agricultural customers? ☐ No ☐ Yes

PART 6 – WITHHOLDING TAX

This is where you can select your filing frequency, the state will review it and could change it based on your reported tax amounts

1. Reason for Kansas withholding tax registration (check all that apply; see instructions)
   ☐ Withholding on wages; taxable payments other than wages; or pensions
   ☐ Withholding on Kansas taxable income of nonresident partners, shareholders

2. Date you began making payments _____ *Skip to Part 12 as indicated in the instructions*

3. Estimate your annual Kansas withholding
   ☐ $200 & under (annual filer)   ☐ $201 - $1,200 (quarterly filer)   ☐ $1,201 - $8,000 (monthly filer)   ☐ $8,001 - $45,000 (semi-monthly filer)

4. If your withholding reports and returns are prepared by a payroll service, complete the following information about the payroll company:
   Name: _____ EIN: ___ ___ - ___ ___ ___ ___ ___ ___ ___ Phone: ( ) _____
   Address: _____ City _____ State _____ Zip Code _____
   10

Kansas – continued.

ENTER YOUR EIN: ____ - _____   OR   SSN: _____ - ____ - _____

PART 7 – CORPORATE INCOME TAX OR PRIVILEGE TAX

1. Date corporation began doing business in Kansas or deriving income from sources within Kansas: ____ / ____ / ____

2. What name and EIN will you be using to report federal income/expenses (if different than in Part 3, questions 2 and 6)?
   Name: _____ EIN: ____ - _____

3. If your business is a financial institution, check the appropriate box: ☐ Bank   ☐ Savings and Loan

4. Check type of tax year: ☐ Calendar Year   ☐ Fiscal Year   If fiscal year, provide year-end date: Month_____ Day _____

5. If your business is a cooperative or political subdivision, check the appropriate box: ☐ Cooperative ☐ Political Subdivision

PART 8 – LIQUOR ENFORCEMENT TAX

1. Date of first sale of alcoholic liquor: ____ / ____ / ____

2. Check type of license: ☐ Liquor Store   ☐ Distributor   ☐ Microbrewery   ☐ Farm Winery
   ☐ Farm Winery Outlet   ☐ Farmers Market Sales Permit   ☐ Special Order Shipping

PART 9 – LIQUOR DRINK TAX

1. Date of first sale of alcoholic beverages: ____ / ____ / ____

2. Check type of license:

   ☐ Class "A" Club   ☐ Class "B" Club   ☐ Caterer   ☐ Hotel (Entire premises)
   ☐ Hotel/Caterer   ☐ Drinking Establishment   ☐ Drinking Establishment/Caterer

PART 10 – CIGARETTE AND TOBACCO TAX

1. Do you make retail sales of cigarettes over-the-counter, by mail, by phone, or over the internet? ☐ No ☐ Yes If yes, you must enclose with this application, a check or money order for $25.00 for each location and provide your e-mail or web page address:
   _____

2. Will you be the operator of cigarette vending machines? ☐ No ☐ Yes If yes, you must enclose Form CG-83 and list the serial number, location address, and manufacturer's brand name of each machine. Also, enclose a check or money order for $25.00 for each machine.

3. Name of company/corporation with whom you have a fuel supply agreement and make retail sale of cigarette and tobacco products (e.g., Shell, BP, Phillips 66, Conoco): _____

4. Name of company/corporation with whom you have a retailing agreement and make retail sale of cigarette and tobacco products (e.g., Shell, BP, Phillips 66, Conoco): _____

PART 11 – NONRESIDENT CONTRACTOR   (See instructions)

If registering for more than one contract, enclose a separate page for each contract.

1. Total amount of this contract: $ _____

2. Required bond: ☐ $1,000   ☐ 8% of Contract   ☐ 4% of Contract (Enclose a copy of the project exemption certificate)

3. List who contract is with: _____   Phone Number: _____

4. Location of Kansas project: _____
   (Street Address)   (City)   (County)

5. Starting date of contract: ____ / ____ / ____

   Estimated contract completion date: ____ / ____ / ____

6. Subcontractor's name (If more than one, please enclose an additional page): _____

   _____
   (Street Address)   (City)   (State)   (Zip Code)

7. Subcontractor's EIN: _____ - _____

8. Subcontractor's portion of contract: $ _____

Kansas – continued.

ENTER YOUR EIN: ___ ___ - ___ ___ ___ ___ ___ ___ ___   <u>OR</u>   SSN: ___ ___ ___ - ___ ___ - ___ ___ ___ ___

PART 12 – OWNERSHIP DISCLOSURE AND SIGNATURE STATEMENT

List ALL owners, partners, corporate officers and directors. Provide the personal information and signatures of all persons who have control or authority over how business funds or assets are spent. If more space is needed, attach additional pages.

Certification: To the best of my knowledge and belief the information on this application is true, correct, and complete. If the business fails to report or pay appropriate state taxes, any individual who is responsible for the tax authorizes the Secretary of Revenue or his/her designee to research the credit history of the business or that individual.

X _____

_____
Printed full proper name of owner, partner or corporate officer

Signature of owner, partner or corporate officer   Date

SSN: _____   Title: _____

Home Address: _____
(Street Address)   (City)   (State)   (Zip Code)

Home Telephone: (___) _____   Email Address: _____   Percent of Ownership: ___%

Do you have control or authority over how business funds or assets are spent? ☐ Yes ☐ No

Date that you became the owner, partner or corporate officer of this business: Month _____ Day _____ Year _____

X _____

_____
Printed full proper name of owner, partner or corporate officer

Signature of owner, partner or corporate officer   Date

SSN: _____   Title: _____

Home Address: _____
(Street Address)   (City)   (State)   (Zip Code)

Home Telephone: (___) _____   Email Address: _____   Percent of Ownership: ___%

Do you have control or authority over how business funds or assets are spent? ☐ Yes ☐ No

Date that you became the owner, partner or corporate officer of this business: Month _____ Day _____ Year _____

X _____

_____
Printed full proper name of owner, partner or corporate officer

Signature of owner, partner or corporate officer   Date

SSN: _____   Title: _____

Home Address: _____
(Street Address)   (City)   (State)   (Zip Code)

Home Telephone: (___) _____   Email Address: _____   Percent of Ownership: ___%

Do you have control or authority over how business funds or assets are spent? ☐ Yes ☐ No

Date that you became the owner, partner or corporate officer of this business: Month _____ Day _____ Year _____

X _____

_____
Printed full proper name of owner, partner or corporate officer

Signature of owner, partner or corporate officer   Date

SSN: _____   Title: _____

Home Address: _____
(Street Address)   (City)   (State)   (Zip Code)

Home Telephone: (___) _____   Email Address: _____   Percent of Ownership: ___%

Do you have control or authority over how business funds or assets are spent? ☐ Yes ☐ No

Date that you became the owner, partner or corporate officer of this business: Month _____ Day _____ Year _____

Send this form and any payments to: Kansas Department of Revenue, 915 SW Harrison St., Topeka, KS 66625-9000 or fax to: (785) 291-3614.
For assistance call (785) 368-8222.

Please visit e-ComSalesTax.com for more information

Kentucky

KENTUCKY TAX REGISTRATION APPLICATION

- Incomplete or illegible applications will delay processing and will be returned.
- Print or type the application using blue or black ink only.
- Please see instructions for questions regarding completion of the application.
- *Need Help?* Call (502) 564-3306 or visit www.revenue.ky.gov

FOR OFFICE USE ONLY		
CRIS	Coded	
CTS CASE#	Date Coded	
CTS Person ID #	Data Entry	
NAICS	SIC	Date Data Entered

SECTION A — REASON FOR COMPLETING THIS APPLICATION (Must Be Completed)

1. **Effective Date** ___ / ___ / ___
   - ☐ Opened new business
   - ☐ Resumption of business
   - ☐ Hired employees working in Kentucky
   - ☐ Hired employees working out-of-state with a KY residence
   - ☐ Applying for additional tax accounts/Began new taxable activity
   - ☐ Bidding for State Government Contract (State Vendor or Affiliates)
   - ☐ Other *(Specify)* _____

   Change in Ownership
   - ☐ Ownership type change—Previous type _____
   - ☐ Purchased an existing business *(See Instructions)*

   To update information for your existing account(s) or report opening a new location of your current business, use Form 10A104, *Update or Cancellation of Kentucky Tax Accounts.*

2. **Previous Account Numbers** *(If Applicable)*
   - Kentucky Withholding Tax _____
   - Kentucky Sales and Use Tax _____
   - Kentucky Corporation Income Tax _____
   - Kentucky Limited Liability Entity Tax _____
   - Kentucky Coal Severance Tax _____
   - Federal ID Number (FEIN) _____

3. **Current Account Numbers** *(If Applicable)*
   - Kentucky Withholding Tax _____
   - Kentucky Sales and Use Tax _____
   - Kentucky Corporation Income Tax _____
   - Kentucky Limited Liability Entity Tax _____
   - Kentucky Coal Severance Tax _____

SECTION B — BUSINESS / RESPONSIBLE PARTY / CONTACT INFORMATION (Must Be Completed)

4. **Legal Business Name** ABC Toys, LLC
5. **Doing Business As** *(See Instructions)* ABC Toys
6. **Federal Employer Identification Number (FEIN)** (Required, complete prior to submitting)
   ☐☐☐ – ☐☐☐☐☐☐☐
7. **Kentucky Secretary of State Organization Number** (If applicable)
   ☐☐☐☐☐☐☐

8. **Business Location**

9. **Location of Business Records**
   - ☐ Use the same address as listed in Item 8

> Most will need to check this box

Street Address *(DO NOT List a PO Box)*			Street Address *(DO NOT List a PO Box)*		
City	State	Zip Code	City	State	Zip Code
Telephone Number ( ) –	County (if in Kentucky)		Telephone Number ( ) –	County (if in Kentucky)	

10. **Accounting Period** ☐ Calendar Year (year ending December 31st) ☐ Fiscal Year (year ending ___ / ___ (mm/dd))

11. **Ownership Type**
    - ☐ Sole Proprietorship
    - ☐ General Partnership
    - ☐ Corporation
    - ☐ S Corporation
    - ☐ Government
    - ☐ Association
    - ☐ Homeowner's Association
    - ☐ Joint Venture
    - ☐ Trust
    - ☐ Non-Profit
    - ☐ Real Estate Investment Trust
    - ☐ Estate
    - ☐ Limited Partnership
    - ☐ Limited Liability Partnership (LLP or LLLP)
    - ☐ Limited Liability Company (LLC)
    - ☐ Cooperative
    - ☐ Other *(See Instructions)*

12. **If "LIMITED LIABILITY COMPANY" is Checked Above, How Will You be Taxed for Federal Purposes?**
    - ☐ A. Partnership
    - ☐ B. Corporation
    - ☐ C. S Corporation
    - ☐ D. Non-Profit
    - ■ Single Member-Disregarded Entity, member taxed as:
      - ☐ E. Individual
      - ☐ F. Other *(Specify)* _____

> Very important because state will expect a Corporate Income tax return if not included in personal return

13–14. OWNERSHIP DISCLOSURE–RESPONSIBLE PARTIES *(REQUIRED FOR ALL OWNERSHIP TYPES)*

Full Legal Name (Last, First, Middle)			Full Legal Name (Last, First, Middle)		
Residence Address			Residence Address		
City	State	Zip Code	City	State	Zip Code
Social Security Number (REQUIRED)	Telephone Number ( ) –		Social Security Number (REQUIRED)	Telephone Number ( ) –	
Business Title		Effective Date of Title	Business Title		Effective Date of Title

> If you omit this, the application will be rejected or you will receive a call to submit this information

15. **Person to contact regarding this application:**

Name (Last, First, Middle)	Title	Daytime Telephone ( ) –	Extension
E-mail: (By supplying your e-mail address you give the Department of Revenue permission to contact you via E-mail.)			

Kentucky – continued.

SECTION C   TELL US ABOUT YOUR BUSINESS OR ORGANIZATION (Must Be Completed)

16. A. Describe the nature of your business activity in Kentucky, including any services provided.

    Online retail sales to end users

    B. If you make sales in Kentucky, list the products sold.

    C. Describe the nature of your business activity outside Kentucky, including any services provided.

> Most will answer "no" to these questions

		Yes	No
17.	Do you have or will you hire employees to work in Kentucky within the next 6 months? (An employee is anyone to whom you pay wages, including part-time help and family members.)	☐	☐
18.	Do you wish to voluntarily withhold on Kentucky residents who work outside Kentucky or withhold on pension and retirement plans?	☐	☐
19.	If your business is a corporation or limited liability company choosing taxation as a corporation for Federal purposes, will the Kentucky officers receive compensation other than dividends?	☐	☐

If you answered "YES" to ANY of questions 17 through 19, you must complete SECTION D.

		Yes	No
20.	Will you make retail and/or wholesale sales of tangible personal property or digital property in Kentucky? (Examples: prepared food, Internet sales, downloaded music and books. See Instructions for more.)	☐	☐
21.	Will you repair, install replacement parts, produce, fabricate, process, print or imprint tangible personal property? (Examples: automotive repairs and window tinting, sign making, embroidery, and engraving. See Instructions for more.)	☐	☐
22.	Will you rent/lease tangible personal property to others, including related companies?	☐	☐
23.	Will you charge taxable admissions?	☐	☐
24.	Will you rent temporary lodging to others?	☐	☐
25.	Will you sell for or are you a manufacturer's agent soliciting orders for a nonresident seller not registered in Kentucky?	☐	☐
26.	Will you receive receipts from the breeding of a stallion to a mare in Kentucky?	☐	☐
27.	Will you make sales of motor vehicles to residents of AZ, CA, FL, IN, MA, MI, SC, or WA?	☐	☐
28.	Will you make sales of aviation/jet fuel?	☐	☐
29.	Are you a manufacturing fee processor or a contract miner located in Kentucky?	☐	☐

> You should answer "YES" to this question

30. Will you sell any of the following?

Yes	No		Yes	No	
☐	☐	A. Coal or other minerals	☐	☐	E. Sewer services
☐	☐	B. Water utilities	☐	☐	F. Communication s...
☐	☐	C. Natural, artifical, or mixed gas	☐	☐	G. Multichannel video programming services*
☐	☐	D. Electricity			*(see Instructions)

If you answered "YES" to ANY of questions 20 through 30 (except 30 G), you must complete SECTION E and you may SKIP questions 31 and 32.

If you answered "YES" to ANY of questions 30 B through 30 G, you must ALSO complete SECTION H.

		Yes	No
31.	Are you a construction company/contractor that will bring into this state construction materials or supplies on which no Kentucky sales tax or equivalent has been paid?	☐	☐
32.	Will you make purchases from out-of-state vendors and not pay Kentucky sales or use tax to the seller on those purchases? (IF YOU ARE A PROFESSIONAL SERVICE BUSINESS, PLEASE SEE INSTRUCTIONS FOR IMPORTANT ADDITIONAL DETAILS)	☐	☐

If you answered "YES" to EITHER of questions 31 or 32, you must complete SECTION F.

		Yes	No
33.	Is your business/organization a corporation, S corporation, professional service corporation, limited partnership (LP), limited liability partnership (LLP or LLLP), professional limited liability partnership (PLLP or PLLLP), limited liability company (LLC), professional limited liability company (PLLC), association, homeowners' association, real estate investment trust (REIT), regulated investment company (RIC), real estate mortgage investment conduit (REMIC), or similar entity created with limited liability for the partners, members or shareholders?	☐	☐

If you answered "YES" to question 33, you MUST answer questions 34 through 41.

Sole Proprietorships and General Partnerships may SKIP questions 34 through 41.

		Yes	No
34.	Is your corporation incorporated or limited liability entity organized under the laws of Kentucky with the Kentucky Secretary of State's Office?	☐	☐
35.	Will your corporation/limited liability entity have its commercial domicile in Kentucky?	☐	☐
36.	Will your corporation/limited liability entity own/lease any real or tangible personal property located in Kentucky?	☐	☐
37.	Will your corporation/limited liability entity have one or more individuals performing services in Kentucky?	☐	☐
38.	Will your corporation/limited liability entity maintain an interest in a pass-through entity doing business in Kentucky?	☐	☐
39.	Will your corporation/limited liability entity derive income from or attributable to sources within Kentucky, including income derived directly/indirectly from a trust/single member limited liability company doing business in Kentucky?	☐	☐
40.	Will your corporation/limited liability entity direct activities at Kentucky customers for the purpose of selling them goods or services?	☐	☐
41.	Will your corporation/limited liability entity own/lease any intangible property or receive payments from a related member as defined in KRS 141.205(1)(g) or an unrelated party for the use of intangible property in Kentucky such as royalties, franchise agreements, patents, trademarks, etc.?	☐	☐

If you answered "YES" to ANY of questions 34 through 41, you MUST complete SECTION G.

		Yes	No
42.	Will you mine coal that you own or possess the mineral rights to, either by deed, lease, consent, etc.?	☐	☐
43.	Does your company perform one or more of the following activities:		
	A. Purchase coal for the purpose of processing and resale?	☐	☐
	B. Process refuse coal?	☐	☐
	(Processing means cleaning, breaking, sizing, dust allaying, treating to prevent freezing, or loading or unloading for any purpose.)		
	C. Purchase and sell coal as a coal broker?	☐	☐

If you answered "YES" to EITHER of questions 42 or 43, you must complete SECTION E and SECTION I.

Kentucky – continued.

FOR OFFICE USE ONLY					
WH #	SU # or USE #	CP/LLET #	TELECOM #	UGRLT #	CT #

SECTION D — EMPLOYER'S WITHHOLDING TAX ACCOUNT
Must be completed if you answered "YES" to ANY of the questions 17 through 19.

44. Number of Kentucky employees _____

45. Date wages/pensions first paid or will be paid (REQUIRED)

    __ __ / __ __ / __ __ __ __

46. Estimated annual withholding in Kentucky:
    - ☐ $0.00–$399.99
    - ☐ $2,000.00–$49,999.99
    - ☐ $400.00–$1,999.99
    - ☐ $50,000.00 or more

47. *Employer's Withholding Tax* returns should be mailed to:
    - ☐ Use the same address as listed on Page 1, Section B, Item 8

c/o or Attn.

Address

City   State   Zip Code

Mailing Telephone Number   County (if in Kentucky)
(   )   -

SECTION E — SALES AND USE TAX ACCOUNT
TRANSIENT ROOM TAX ACCOUNT AND MOTOR VEHICLE TIRE FEE ACCOUNT
Must be completed if you answered "YES" to ANY of the questions 20 through 30 (except 30 G).

48. Date sales began or will begin (REQUIRED)

    __ __ / __ __ / __ __ __ __

    most small businesses are cash

49. Accounting Method ☐ Cash   ☐ Accrual

50. Do you rent temporary lodging to others? ☐ Yes   ☐ No

51. Do you sell new tires for motor vehicles? ☐ Yes   ☐ No

52. Estimated gross monthly sales tax in Kentucky:
    - ☐ $0.00–$1,199.99
    - ☐ $1,200.00 or more

    for use in determining filing frequency

53. *Sales and Use Tax* returns should be mailed to:
    - ☐ Use the same address as listed on Page 1, Section B, Item 8

c/o or Attn.

Address

City   State   Zip Code

County (if in Kentucky)

SECTION F — CONSUMER'S USE TAX ACCOUNT
Must be completed if you answered "YES" to EITHER question 31 or 32.

54. Date purchases began or will begin (REQUIRED)

    __ __ / __ __ / __ __ __ __

    * If you make a one-time purchase only, see the instructions

55. *Consumer's Use Tax* returns should be mailed to:
    - ☐ Use the same address as listed on Page 1, Section B, Item 8

c/o or Attn.

Address

City   State   Zip Code

Mailing Telephone Number   County (if in Kentucky)
(   )   -

SECTION G — CORPORATION INCOME AND/OR LIMITED LIABILITY ENTITY TAX ACCOUNT
Must be completed if you answered "YES" to ANY of the questions 34 through 41.

56. Date of Incorporation or organization
    __ __ / __ __ / __ __ __ __

57. State of Incorporation or organization _____

58. Date of qualification with the Kentucky Secretary of State's Office
    __ __ / __ __ / __ __ __ __

59. If a foreign entity, date that activity or receipt of pass through income began or will begin in Kentucky.
    __ __ / __ __ / __ __ __ __

60. If a foreign entity, is your Kentucky activity limited to the mere solicitation of the sale of tangible personal property? ☐ Yes   ☐ No

61. Is your entity an exempt organization under Kentucky law?
    ☐ Yes   ☐ No
    If yes, list the exemption type: _____

62. *Corporation Income and/or Limited Liability Entity Tax* returns should be mailed to:
    - ☐ Use the same address as listed on Page 1, Section B, Item 8

c/o or Attn.

Address

City   State   Zip Code

Mailing Telephone Number   County (if in Kentucky)
(   )   -

Please visit e-ComSalesTax.com for more information

Kentucky – continued.

SECTION H	TELECOMMUNICATIONS TAX ACCOUNT AND/OR UTILITY GROSS RECEIPTS LICENSE TAX ACCOUNT
	Must be completed if you answered "YES" to ANY questions 30 B through 30 G.

63. Date sales of communications or utilities began or will begin (REQUIRED)

_ _ _ / SKIP _____ →

64. Telephone

(_____) _____ - _____

Once the account for *Telecommunications Tax* is assigned, use the following web site to set up account for filing of returns.
http://revenue.ky.gov/business/Telecom.htm

Once the account for *Utility Gross Receipts License Tax* is assigned, use the following web site to set up account for filing of returns.
http://revenue.ky.gov/business/utilschool.htm

SECTION I	COAL SEVERANCE/PROCESSING TAX ACCOUNT and/or COAL SELLER/PURCHASER CERTIFICATE ID #
	Must be completed if you answered "YES" to EITHER question 42 or 43.

65. Date mining/processing or coal brokering operations began or will begin (REQUIRED)

_ _ / _ _ / _ _ _ _   SKIP

66. *Coal Severance & Processing Tax* returns should be mailed to:

☐ Use the same address as listed on Page 1, Section B, Item 9

c/o or Attn.		
Address		
City	State	Zip Code
Mailing Telephone Number ( ) -	County (if in Kentucky)	

IMPORTANT: THIS APPLICATION MUST BE SIGNED BELOW:

The statements contained in this application and any accompanying schedules are hereby certified to be correct to the best knowledge and belief of the undersigned who is duly authorized to sign the application.

Signed: _____

Phone Number: _____

Title: _____ Date: ___/___/___ (mm/dd/yyyy)

Signed: _____

Phone Number: _____

Title: _____ Date: ___/___/___ (mm/dd/yyyy)

For assistance in completing the application, please call the **Taxpayer Registration Section** at **(502) 564-3306**, Monday through Friday between the hours of 8:00 a.m. and 5:00 p.m., Eastern time, or you may contact one of the Kentucky Taxpayer Service Centers or use the Telecommunications Device for the Deaf. Each office is open Monday through Friday, 8:00 a.m. to 5:00 p.m., local time. For a list of Taxpayer Service Centers and phone numbers, see the Instructions.

MAIL completed application to: **KENTUCKY DEPARTMENT OF REVENUE**   or   **FAX to:**   **502-227-0772**
P.O. BOX 299, STATION 20
FRANKFORT, KENTUCKY 40602-0299

See Form 10A100-I, Instructions for Kentucky Tax Registration Application, for step-by-step instructions and additional information in completing this application.

If you are applying for a withholding account and/or a sales and use tax account and would like to receive a packet to register for Electronic Funds Transfer (EFT), please call (502) 564-6020.

To register for cigarette tax, minerals or natural gas severance tax, motor fuels tax, or any other miscellaneous taxes or fees administered by the Department of Revenue, please visit the Department's Web site at www.revenue.ky.gov.

This form does not include registration with the Secretary of State, Unemployment Insurance, or Workers' Compensation Insurance. For assistance please contact those offices at the numbers below.

Secretary of State	(502) 564-3490	Unemployment Insurance	(502) 564-2272	Workers' Compensation	(502) 564-5550
IRS--FEIN	(800) 829-4933				

For assistance with other questions about starting a business in Kentucky, including special licensing and permitting requirements, business structure registration, employer responsibilities, and business development resources, visit the Business Information Clearinghouse online at www.thinkkentucky.com/BIC or call toll free 1-800-626-2250.

The Kentucky Department of Revenue does not discriminate on the basis of race, color, national origin, sex, religion, age or disability in employment or the provision of services.

Please visit e-ComSalesTax.com for more information

NEVADA BUSINESS REGISTRATION

Important details are included in the instructions. Please type or print legibly in black ink. Each agency may request additional information depending on your type of business. Completing this form does not relieve you of any statutory or regulatory requirements relating to your business. Online registration is also available. See instructions.

1	I Am Applying For: * SEND A COPY TO EACH AGENCY	☐ Unemployment Insurance *(Employment Security Division – ESD)	☐ Sales/Use Tax Permit *(Department of Taxation)	☐ Modified Business Tax	☐ Local Business License
2	☐ New Business	☐ Change In Ownership/ Business Entity ☐ Change In Corporate Officers ☐ Change In Name	☐ Change In Location ☐ Change In Mailing Address ☐ Add Location		☐ Other
3	Business Entity Type:	☐ Sole Proprietor ☐ Publicly Traded Corp ☐ Association ☐ Limited Liability Partnership ☐ Government Entity ☐ S Corp. ☐ Privately Held Corp ☐ Partnership ☐ Limited Liability Company ☐ Other			

4	Corporate/Entity Name (as shown on State Business License): ABC Toys, LLC ← legal name	5	Corporate/Entity Telephone	Federal Tax Identification Number
6	Corporate/Entity Address:	Street Number, Direction (N, S, E, W) and Name Suite, Unit or Apt # City, State, and Zip Code +4		State of Incorporation or Formation

7	Nevada Name (DBA): ABC Toys	Business Telephone	Fax
8	E-mail Address:	Website Address:	9	Nevada Business Identification # (11 digits) NV
10	Mailing Address:	Street Number, Direction (N, S, E, W) and Name Suite, Unit or Apt # City, State, and Zip Code +4
11	Location(s) of Nevada Business Operations:	Street Number, Direction ~~do not put~~ Apt # City, State, and Zip Code +4
12	Location of Business Records:	Street Number, Direction ~~Amazon's location~~ Apt # City, State, and Zip Code +4 Telephone Number:

13 List All Owners, Partners, Corporate Officers, Managers, Members, etc. (If individual ownership, list only one owner.) Attach Additional Sheets If Needed. ** The Department of Taxation & Employment Security Division are the only agencies to require a SSN.

Last, First, MI:	Residence Address (Street)	**SSN	Date of Birth
Title	Percent Owned 0%	City, State, Zip +4		Residence Telephone
Last, First, MI:	Residence Address (Street)	**SSN	Date of Birth
Title	Percent Owned 0%	City, State, Zip +4		Residence Telephone
Last, First, MI:	Residence Address (Street)	**SSN	Date of Birth
Title	Percent Owned 0%	City, State, Zip +4		Residence Telephone
Responsible Local Contact (Last, First, MI & Title):	Residence Address (Street), City, State, Zip +4	**SSN	Residence Telephone

14	Date Business Started in Nevada	Date Nevada Location Opened	Date First Worker Hired in Nevada	Date of First Nevada Payroll	Amount of First Nevada Payroll	Number of Employees

15 PLEASE CHECK ALL THAT APPLY TO YOUR BUSINESS

☐ Mining	☐ Domestics	☐ Outside Dining	☐ Water Appropriation	☐ Adult Materials/Activity	☐ Amusement Machines	☐ Registered Agent
☐ Service	☐ Agriculture	☐ Home Occupation	☐ Hazardous Material	☐ Leased or Leasing Employees	☐ Alcohol	☐ Financial Institutions
☐ Tobacco	☐ Manufacturing	☐ Retail Sales—New	☐ Construction/Erection	☐ Leasing (Other than Employees)	☐ Gaming	☐ Mortgage Brokers
☐ Delivery	☐ Transportation	☐ Retail Sales—Used	☐ Tire Sales	☐ Supply/Use Temporary Workers	☐ Health Services	☐ Banker
☐ Wholesale	☐ Not for Profit	☐ Live Entertainment	☐ Environmental Discharge	☐ Regulated by Federal/State Permit Number.		☐ Other:

16 Describe in Detail the Nature of Your Business in Nevada. Include Product Sold, Labor Performed and/or Services Rendered. State the approximate percentage of sales or revenues resulting from each item. Example: Retail sale of major appliances to public 60%; repair 40%.

Online retail sales of new and used books, games, toys, tools, etc. - 100%

17 If You Have Acquired A Nevada Business, Changed Ownership/Business Entity, or Have a New Federal Tax Number, Complete This Section:

Date Acquired/Changed:	Acquired/Changed by: ☐ Purchase ☐ Lease ☐ Other	Portion Acquired/Changed: ☐ In Whole ☐ In Part
Name(s) of Previous Owner(s)	Previous Owner(s) Business Name	
Address (Street)	City	State Zip Code +4
Enter Your Previous Nevada Sales/Use Tax Permit Number, if applicable:	Enter Previous Owner(s) ESD Account Number:	

18 * Signatures must be that of a responsible party *
I declare under penalty of perjury that the information provided is true, correct and complete to the best of my knowledge and belief and acknowledge that pursuant to NRS 239.330, it is a category C felony to knowingly offer any false or forged instrument for filing.

*Signature Responsible Party / Original	Print Name And Title	Date
*Signature Responsible Party / Original	Print Name And Title	Date

ORIGINAL SIGNATURES REQUIRED BY AGENCIES – KEEP A COPY FOR YOUR RECORDS

Please visit e-ComSalesTax.com for more information

Nevada – continued.

<table>
<tr><td colspan="2"></td><td colspan="2">For Department Use Only</td></tr>
<tr><td colspan="2">**NEVADA DEPARTMENT OF TAXATION**</td><td colspan="2">TID:</td></tr>
<tr><td colspan="2">**SUPPLEMENTAL REGISTRATION**
Please print clearly — Use black or blue ink only
Please mark applicable type(s) (See Instructions)</td><td colspan="2">Dept. of Taxation Representative accepting application:</td></tr>
</table>

☐ Sales/Use Permit   ☐ Consumers Certificate   ☐ Certificate of Authority   ☐ Live Entertainment Tax

1. DBA (as shown on the Nevada Business Registration Form):
ABC Toys

2. Business telephone number: **3.** List STATE of incorporation or formation if applicable:

4. FEES AND SECURITY DEPOSIT

5. Estimated total monthly receipts: **6.** Estimated total Nevada monthly TAXABLE receipts:

7. Reporting cycle (check choice of reporting)
Sales Tax Accounts with over $10,000 a month in TAXABLE sales must report monthly.

pick your desired reporting cycle

	Monthly	Quarterly	Annual
Sales/Use Tax	☐	☐	
Use Tax	☐	☐	☐
Live Entertainment Tax Occupancy ☐ 200 to 7,499 ☐ 7,500 or More	☐		

8. Security (See Instructions)
☑ Cash $ 0.00   ☐ Surety # _____

9. Sales Tax Fee (See instructions):   **10.** Total Nevada Business Locations:

11. OTHER INFORMATION

Name of spouse/relative	Address of spouse/relative	Phone number of spouse/relative
Name of other contact	Address of other contact	Phone number of other contact
Accountant/bookkeeper	Address of accountant/bookkeeper	Phone number of accountant/bookkeeper

Other employment (If applicable):
Company name: Company name:

Name of bank/financial institution – location / account number:
Business account:
Personal account:

FOR DEPARTMENT USE ONLY

ST/UT No.: _____   MBT No.: _____

Combine Accts: ☐ Yes ☐ No   Previous Acct: _____   Previous Acct Cancelled: ☐ Yes ☐ No

Comments: _____

☐ Cash   ☐ Check   ABA #: _____   Bank: _____   Branch: _____

**For an introduction to the Department and general information, see our Taxpayer Information Packet Online at www.tax.state.nv.us **

PA-100 (03-09)

MAIL COMPLETED APPLICATION TO:
DEPARTMENT OF REVENUE
BUREAU OF BUSINESS TRUST FUND TAXES
PO BOX 280901
HARRISBURG, PA 17128-0901

COMMONWEALTH OF PENNSYLVANIA
PA ENTERPRISE
REGISTRATION FORM

DEPARTMENT USE ONLY

RECEIVED DATE

DEPARTMENT OF REVENUE &
DEPARTMENT OF LABOR AND INDUSTRY

TYPE OR PRINT LEGIBLY, USE BLACK INK

SECTION 1 – REASON FOR THIS REGISTRATION

REFER TO THE INSTRUCTIONS (PAGE 16) AND CHECK THE APPLICABLE BOX(ES) TO INDICATE THE REASON(S) FOR THIS REGISTRATION.

1. ☐ NEW REGISTRATION
2. ☐ ADDING TAX(ES) & SERVICE(S)
3. ☐ REACTIVATING TAX(ES) & SERVICE(S)
4. ☐ ADDING ESTABLISHMENT(S)
5. ☐ INFORMATION UPDATE

6. DID THIS ENTERPRISE:
☐ YES ☐ NO ACQUIRE ALL OR PART OF ANOTHER BUSINESS?
☐ YES ☐ NO RESULT FROM A CHANGE IN LEGAL STRUCTURE (FOR EXAMPLE, FROM INDIVIDUAL PROPRIETOR TO CORPORATION, PARTNERSHIP TO CORPORATION, CORPORATION TO LIMITED LIABILITY COMPANY, ETC)?
☐ YES ☐ NO UNDERGO A MERGER, CONSOLIDATION, DISSOLUTION, OR OTHER RESTRUCTURING?

SECTION 2 – ENTERPRISE INFORMATION

1. DATE OF FIRST OPERATIONS
2. DATE OF FIRST OPERATIONS IN PA
3. ENTERPRISE FISCAL YEAR END

can be calendar year end

4. ENTERPRISE LEGAL NAME
5. FEDERAL EMPLOYER IDENTIFICATION NUMBER (EIN)

6. ENTERPRISE TRADE NAME (if different than legal name)
7. ENTERPRISE TELEPHONE NUMBER ( )

8. ENTERPRISE STREET ADDRESS (do not use PO Box) | CITY/TOWN | COUNTY | STATE | ZIP CODE + 4

9. ENTERPRISE MAILING ADDRESS (if different than street address) | CITY/TOWN | STATE | ZIP CODE + 4

10. LOCATION OF ENTERPRISE RECORDS (street address) | CITY/TOWN

Probably "N/A" for most online sellers

11. ESTABLISHMENT NAME (doing business as) | 12. NUMBER OF ESTABLISHMENTS * | 13. PA SCHOOL DISTRICT | 14. PA MUNICIPALITY

* ENTERPRISES WITH ONE OR MORE ESTABLISHMENTS WITHIN PA, WHOSE PA ADDRESS WAS NOT ENTERED ABOVE, MUST COMPLETE SECTION 17. (SEE GENERAL INSTRUCTIONS AND SECTION 17 FOR MORE INFORMATION.)

SECTION 3 – TAXES AND SERVICES

ALL REGISTRANTS MUST CHECK THE APPLICABLE BOX(ES) TO INDICATE THE TAX(ES) AND SERVICE(S) REQUESTED FOR THIS REGISTRATION AND COMPLETE THE CORRESPONDING SECTIONS INDICATED ON PAGES 2 AND 3. IF REACTIVATING ANY PREVIOUS ACCOUNT(S), LIST THE ACCOUNT NUMBER(S) IN THE SPACE PROVIDED.

PREVIOUS ACCOUNT NUMBER

PREVIOUS ACCOUNT NUMBER

☐ CIGARETTE DEALER'S LICENSE
☐ CORPORATION TAXES
☐ EMPLOYER WITHHOLDING TAX
☐ FUELS TAX PERMIT
☐ LIQUID FUELS TAX PERMIT
☐ MOTOR CARRIERS ROAD TAX/IFTA
☐ PROMOTER LICENSE
☐ PUBLIC TRANSPORTATION ASSISTANCE TAX LICENSE
☐ SALES TAX EXEMPT STATUS

☐ SALES, USE, HOTEL OCCUPANCY TAX LICENSE
☐ SMALL GAMES OF CHANCE LIC./CERT.
☐ TRANSIENT VENDOR CERTIFICATE
☐ UNEMPLOYMENT COMPENSATION
☐ USE TAX
☐ VEHICLE RENTAL TAX
☐ WHOLESALER CERTIFICATE
☐ WORKERS' COMPENSATION COVERAGE

PA DOR calls the sales tax all of these, you are obtaining a hotel tax license per se

SECTION 4 – AUTHORIZED SIGNATURE

I, (WE) THE UNDERSIGNED, DECLARE UNDER THE PENALTIES OF PERJURY THAT THE STATEMENTS CONTAINED HEREIN ARE TRUE, CORRECT, AND COMPLETE.

AUTHORIZED SIGNATURE (ATTACH POWER OF ATTORNEY IF APPLICABLE) | DAYTIME TELEPHONE NUMBER ( ) | TITLE

TYPE OR PRINT NAME | E-MAIL ADDRESS | DATE

TYPE OR PRINT PREPARER'S NAME | | TITLE

DAYTIME TELEPHONE NUMBER ( ) | E-MAIL ADDRESS | DATE

Pennsylvania – continued.

ENTERPRISE NAME	DEPARTMENT USE ONLY

SECTION 5 - BUSINESS STRUCTURE

CHECK THE APPROPRIATE BOX FOR QUESTIONS 1, 2 & 3. IN ADDITION TO SECTIONS 1 THROUGH 10, COMPLETE THE SECTION(S) INDICATED.

1. ☐ SOLE PROPRIETORSHIP (INDIVIDUAL) ☐ GENERAL PARTNERSHIP ☐ ASSOCIATION ☐ LIMITED LIABILITY COMPANY
   ☐ CORPORATION (Sec. 11) ☐ LIMITED PARTNERSHIP ☐ BUSINESS TRUST STATE WHERE CHARTERED _____
   ☐ GOVERNMENT (Sec. 13) ☐ LIMITED LIABILITY PARTNERSHIP ☐ ESTATE ☐ RESTRICTED PROFESSIONAL COMPANY
   ☐ JOINT VENTURE PARTNERSHIP STATE WHERE CHARTERED _____

2. ☐ PROFIT ☐ NON-PROFIT IS THE ENTERPRISE ORGANIZED FOR PROFIT OR NON-PROFIT?

3. ☐ YES ☐ NO IS THE ENTERPRISE EXEMPT FROM TAXATION UNDER INTERNAL REVENUE CODE (IRC) SECTION 501(c) (3)? IF YES, PROVIDE A COPY OF THE ENTERPRISE'S EXEMPTION AUTHORIZATION LETTER FROM THE INTERNAL REVENUE SERVICE.

SECTION 6 - OWNERS, PARTNERS, SHAREHOLDERS, OFFICERS, AND RESPONSIBLE PARTY INFORMATION

PROVIDE THE FOLLOWING FOR ALL INDIVIDUAL AND/OR ENTERPRISE OWNERS, PARTNERS, SHAREHOLDERS, OFFICERS, AND RESPONSIBLE PARTIES. IF STOCK IS PUBLICLY TRADED, PROVIDE THE FOLLOWING FOR ANY SHAREHOLDER WITH AN EQUITY POSITION OF 5% OR MORE. ADDITIONAL SPACE IS AVAILABLE IN SECTION 6A, PAGE 11.

1. NAME	2. SOCIAL SECURITY NUMBER	3. DATE OF BIRTH *	4. FEDERAL EIN

5. ☐ OWNER ☐ OFFICER ☐ PARTNER ☐ SHAREHOLDER ☐ RESPONSIBLE PARTY	6. TITLE	7. EFFECTIVE DATE OF TITLE	8. PERCENTAGE OF OWNERSHIP %	9. EFFECTIVE DATE OF OWNERSHIP
10. HOME ADDRESS (street)	CITY/TOWN	COUNTY	STATE	ZIP CODE + 4

11. THIS PERSON IS RESPONSIBLE TO REMIT/MAINTAIN: ☐ SALES TAX ☐ EMPLOYER WITHHOLDING TAX ☐ MOTOR FUEL TAXES
☐ WORKERS' COMPENSA...

← Generally, all states indicate an officer can be personally liable for sales tax if business is not solvent

* DATE OF BIRTH REQUIRED ONLY IF APPLYING FOR A CIGARETTE WHOLESALE DEALER OF CHANCE MANUFACTURER CERTIFICATE.

SECTION 7 - ESTABLISHMENT BUSINESS ACTIVITY INFORMATION

REFER TO THE INSTRUCTIONS ON PAGES 20 & 21 TO COMPLETE THIS SECTION. COMPLETE SECTION 17 FOR MULTIPLE ESTABLISHMENTS.

1. ENTER THE PERCENTAGE THAT EACH PA BUSINESS ACTIVITY REPRESENTS OF THE TOTAL RECEIPTS OR REVENUES AT THIS ESTABLISHMENT. LIST PRODUCTS OR SERVICES ASSOCIATED WITH EACH BUSINESS ACTIVITY AND THE PERCENTAGE REPRESENTING THE TOTAL RECEIPTS OR REVENUES.

PA BUSINESS ACTIVITY	%	PRODUCTS OR SERVICES	%	ADDITIONAL PRODUCTS OR SERVICES	%
Accommodation & Food Services					
Agriculture, Forestry, Fishing, & Hunting					
Art, Entertainment, & Recreation Services					
Communications/Information					
Construction (must complete question 3)					
Domestics (Private Households)					
Educational Services					
Finance					
Health Care Services					
Insurance					
Management, Support & Remediation Services					
Manufacturing					
Mining, Quarrying, & Oil/Gas Extraction					
Other Services					
Professional, Scientific, & Technical Services					
Public Administration					
Real Estate					
Retail Trade					
Sanitary Service					
Social Assistance Services					
Transportation					
Utilities					
Warehousing					
Wholesale Trade					
TOTAL	100%				

2. ENTER THE PERCENTAGE THAT THIS ESTABLISHMENT'S RECEIPTS OR REVENUES REPRESENT OF THE TOTAL PA RECEIPTS OR REVENUES OF THE ENTERPRISE. _____% SINGLE ESTABLISHMENT ENTERPRISES ENTER 100%. MULTIPLE ESTABLISHMENT ENTERPRISES ENTER PERCENTAGE OF ENTERPRISE (SEE SECTION 17).

3. ESTABLISHMENTS ENGAGED IN CONSTRUCTION MUST ENTER THE PERCENTAGE OF CONSTRUCTION ACTIVITY THAT IS NEW AND/OR RENOVATIVE AND THE PERCENTAGE OF CONSTRUCTION ACTIVITY THAT IS RESIDENTIAL AND/OR COMMERCIAL.

_____ % NEW + _____ % RENOVATIVE = 100%
_____ % RESIDENTIAL + _____ % COMMERCIAL = 100%

4. ☐ YES ☐ NO DOES THIS ENTERPRISE WANT TO BECOME A PENNSYLVANIA LOTTERY RETAILER?

Pennsylvania – continued.

PA-100 (03-09)

ENTERPRISE NAME

DEPARTMENT USE ONLY

SECTION 8 – ESTABLISHMENT SALES INFORMATION

1. ☐ YES   ☐ NO   IS THIS ESTABLISHMENT SELLING TAXABLE PRODUCTS OR OFFERING TAXABLE SERVICES TO CONSUMERS FROM A LOCATION IN PENNSYLVANIA? IF YES, COMPLETE SECTION 18.

2. ☐ YES   ☐ NO   IS THIS ESTABLISHMENT SELLING CIGARETTES IN PENNSYLVANIA? IF YES, COMPLETE SECTIONS 18 AND 19.

3. LIST EACH COUNTY IN PENNSYLVANIA WHERE THIS ESTABLISHMENT IS CONDUCTING TAXABLE SALES ACTIVITY(IES).

COUNTY _____   COUNTY _____   COUNTY _____

COUNTY _____   COUNTY _____   COUNTY _____

ATTACH ADDITIONAL 8 1/2 X 11 SHEETS IF NECESSARY.

SECTION 9 – ESTABLISHMENT EMPLOYMENT INFORMATION

PART 1

1. ☐ YES   ☐ NO   DOES THIS ESTABLISHMENT EMPLOY INDIVIDUALS WHO WORK IN PENNSYLVANIA? IF YES, INDICATE:

    a. DATE WAGES FIRST PAID (MM/DD/YYYY) .... _____

    b. DATE WAGES RESUMED FOLLOWING A BREAK IN EMPLOYMENT .... _____

    c. TOTAL NUMBER OF EMPLOYEES .... _____

    d. NUMBER OF EMPLOYEES PRIMARILY WORKING IN NEW BUILDING OR INFRASTRUCTURE .... _____

    e. NUMBER OF EMPLOYEES PRIMARILY WORKING IN REMODELING CONSTRUCTION .... _____

    f. ESTIMATED GROSS WAGES PER QUARTER .... $ _____ .00

    g. NAME OF WORKERS' COMPENSATION INSURANCE COMPANY _____

       1. POLICY NUMBER _____ EFFECTIVE START DATE _____ END DATE _____

       2. AGENCY NAME _____ DAYTIME TELEPHONE NUMBER (___)

       MAILING ADDRESS _____ CITY/TOWN _____ STATE ___ ZIP CODE + 4 _____

       3. IF THIS ENTERPRISE DOES NOT HAVE WORKERS' COMPENSATION INSURANCE, CHECK ONE:

         a. THIS ESTABLISHMENT EMPLOYS ONLY EXCLUDED WORKERS .... ☐

         b. THIS ESTABLISHMENT HAS ZERO EMPLOYEES .... ☐

         c. THIS ESTABLISHMENT RECEIVED APPROVAL TO SELF-INSURE BY THE PA BUREAU OF WORKERS' COMPENSATION .... ☐

         IF ITEM 3c. IS CHECKED, PROVIDE PA WORKERS' COMPENSATION BUREAU CODE _____

> Unless you live in PA, or employee PA residents you can skip this section

2. ☐ YES   ☐ NO   DOES THIS ESTABLISHMENT EMPLOY PA RESIDENTS WHO WORK OUTSIDE OF PENNSYLVANIA? IF YES, INDICATE:

    a. DATE WAGES FIRST PAID (MM/DD/YYYY) .... _____

    b. DATE WAGES RESUMED FOLLOWING A BREAK IN EMPLOYMENT .... _____

    c. ESTIMATED GROSS WAGES PER QUARTER .... $ _____ .00

3. ☐ YES   ☐ NO   DOES THIS ESTABLISHMENT PAY REMUNERATION FOR SERVICES TO PERSONS YOU DO NOT CONSIDER EMPLOYEES? IF YES, EXPLAIN THE SERVICES PERFORMED _____

PART 2

1. ☐ YES   ☐ NO   IS THIS REGISTRATION A RESULT OF A TAXABLE DISTRIBUTION FOR PA RESIDENTS?

IF YES, INDICATE: a. DATE BENEFITS FIRST PAID (MM/DD/YYYY) .... _____

         b. ESTIMATED BENEFITS PAID PER QUARTER .... $ _____ .00

> Unless you purchased an existing business you can skip this section

SECTION 10 – BULK SALE/TRANSFER INFORMATION

IF ASSETS WERE ACQUIRED IN BULK FROM MORE THAN ONE ENTERPRISE, PHOTOCOPY THIS SECTION AND PROVIDE THE FOLLOWING INFORMATION ABOUT EACH SELLER/TRANSFEROR.

1. ☐ YES   ☐ NO   DID THE ENTERPRISE ACQUIRE 51% OR MORE OF ANY CLASS OF THE PA ASSETS OF ANOTHER ENTERPRISE? SEE THE CLASS OF ASSETS LISTED BELOW.

2. ☐ YES   ☐ NO   DID THE ENTERPRISE ACQUIRE 51% OR MORE OF THE TOTAL ASSETS OF ANOTHER ENTERPRISE?

IF THE ANSWER TO EITHER QUESTION IS YES, PROVIDE THE FOLLOWING INFORMATION ABOUT THE SELLER/TRANSFEROR.

3. SELLER/TRANSFEROR NAME			4. FEDERAL EIN	
5. SELLER/TRANSFEROR STREET ADDRESS	CITY/TOWN		STATE	ZIP CODE + 4

6. DATE ASSETS ACQUIRED	7. ASSETS ACQUIRED:			
	☐ ACCOUNTS RECEIVABLE	☐ EQUIPMENT	☐ INVENTORY	☐ NAME AND/OR GOODWILL
	☐ CONTRACTS	☐ FIXTURES	☐ LEASES	☐ REAL ESTATE
	☐ CUSTOMERS/CLIENTS	☐ FURNITURE	☐ MACHINERY	☐ OTHER _____

IMPORTANT: IE IN ADDITION TO ACQUIRING ASSETS IN BULK, THE ENTERPRISE ALSO ACQUIRED ALL OR PART OF A PREDECESSOR'S BUSINESS, SECTION 14 MUST BE COMPLETED. IF THE ENTERPRISE IS ACQUIRING 51% OR MORE OF ANY CLASS OF PA ASSETS AND/OR 51% OF THE TOTAL ASSETS OF ANOTHER ENTERPRISE THE SELLER MUST OBTAIN A BULK SALE CLEARANCE CERTIFICATE. REFER TO INSTRUCTIONS ON PAGE 22.

Pennsylvania – continued.

PA-100 (03-09)

| | Be sure to complete this at the top of each page of your application | BE ONLY |

ENTERPRISE NAME

SECTION 11 – CORPORATION INFORMATION

| 1. DATE OF INCORPORATION | 2. STATE OF INCORPORATION | 3. CERTIFICATE OF AUTHORITY DATE (NON-PA CORP.) | 4. COUNTRY OF INCORPORATION |

5. ☐ YES   ☐ NO   IS THIS CORPORATION'S STOCK PUBLICLY TRADED?

6. CHECK THE APPROPRIATE BOX(ES) TO DESCRIBE THIS CORPORATION:

CORPORATION:	☐ STOCK	☐ PROFESSIONAL	BANK: ☐ STATE	MUTUAL THRIFT: ☐ STATE	INSURANCE ☐ PA
	☐ NON-STOCK	☐ COOPERATIVE	☐ FEDERAL	☐ FEDERAL	COMPANY: ☐ NON-PA
	☐ MANAGEMENT	☐ STATUTORY CLOSE			

Generally can skip this section

7. S CORPORATION: ☐ FEDERAL   IN ACCORDANCE WITH ACT NO.67 OF 2006, A CORPORATION WI... ...IS IS CONSIDERED A PA S COR-PORATION. IN ORDER NOT TO BE TAXED AS A PA S CORPORATION, REV-976 MUST BE FILED. THE FORM CAN BE ACCESSED AT WWW.REVENUE.STATE.PA.US, FORMS AND PUBLICATIONS, CORPORATION TAX.

COMPLETING THIS FORM WILL NOT FULFILL THE REQUIREMENT TO REGISTER FOR CORPORATE TAXES. REGISTERING CORPORATIONS MUST CONTACT THE PA DEPART-MENT OF STATE TO SECURE CORPORATE NAME CLEARANCE AND REGISTER FOR CORPORATION TAX PURPOSES. CONTACT THE PA DEPARTMENT OF STATE AT (717) 787-1057, OR VISIT www.paopenforbusiness.state.pa.us.

SECTION 12 – REPORTING & PAYMENT METHODS

1. THE DEPARTMENT OF REVENUE REQUIRES THAT ANY ENTERPRISE MAKING PAYMENTS EQUAL TO OR GREATER THAN $20,000 REMIT PAYMENTS VIA ONE OF THE FOL-LOWING ELECTRONIC METHODS: ELECTRONIC FUNDS TRANSFER (EFT); ELECTRONIC TAX INFORMATION AND DATA EXCHANGE SYSTEM (e-TIDES); TELEFILE SYSTEM OR CREDIT CARD. AN ENTERPRISE, REGARDLESS OF AMOUNT, IS ENCOURAGED TO REMIT TAX PAYMENTS ELECTRONICALLY.

a. ☐ YES   ☐ NO   DOES THIS ENTERPRISE MEET THE DEPARTMENT OF REVENUE'S REQUIREMENTS FOR ELECTRONIC PAYMENTS?

b. ☐ YES   ☐ NO   DOES THIS ENTERPRISE WANT TO PARTICIPATE IN THE DEPARTMENT OF REVENUE'S ELECTRONIC PROGRAMS?

2. ☐ YES   ☐ NO   IF THIS ENTERPRISE IS A NON-PROFIT ORGANIZATION THAT IS EXEMPT UNDER IRC 501(c)(3), OR POLITICAL SUB-DIVISIONS, IS IT INTERESTED IN RECEIVING INFORMATION ABOUT THE DEPARTMENT OF LABOR & INDUSTRY'S OPTION OF FINANCING UC COSTS UNDER THE REIMBURSEMENT METHOD IN LIEU OF THE CONTRIBUTORY METHOD? FOR MORE DETAILS, REFER TO SECTION 12 INSTRUCTIONS.

THE DEPARTMENT OF LABOR & INDUSTRY REQUIRES THAT ANY ENTERPRISE WITH 250 OR MORE WAGE ENTRIES PER QUARTERLY REPORT, FILE THE WAGE INFORMATION VIA MAGNETIC MEDIA. ANY MAGNETIC REPORTING FILE MUST BE SUBMITTED FOR COMPATIBILITY WITH THE DEPARTMENT OF LABOR & INDUSTRY'S FORMAT. CONTACT THE MAG-NETIC MEDIA REPORTING UNIT AT (717) 783-5802 FOR MORE INFORMATION.

THE COMMONWEALTH STRONGLY RECOMMENDS THAT ENTERPRISES USE ELECTRONIC FILING AND PAYMENT OPTIONS FOR CERTAIN PENNSYLVANIA TAXES AND SERVICES. INFORMATION ABOUT INTERNET FILING OPTIONS CAN BE FOUND ON THE e-TIDES WEBSITE AT www.etides.state.pa.us.

If this applies you will be required to e-file

SECTION 13 – GOVERNMENT STRUCTURE

1. IS THE ENTERPRISE A:

☐ GOVERNMENT BODY   ☐ GOVERNMENT OWNED ENTERPRISE   ☐ GOVERNMENT & PRIVATE SECTOR OWNED ENTERPRISE

2. IS THE GOVERNMENT:

☐ DOMESTIC/USA   ☐ FOREIGN/NON-USA   ☐ MULTI-NATIONAL

3. IF DOMESTIC, IS THE GOVERNMENT:

☐ FEDERAL	LOCAL: ☐ COUNTY	☐ BOROUGH
☐ STATE GOVERNOR'S JURISDICTION	☐ CITY	☐ SCHOOL DISTRICT
☐ STATE NON-GOVERNOR'S JURISDICTION	☐ TOWN	☐ OTHER _____
	☐ TOWNSHIP	

Pennsylvania – continued.

PA-100 (03-09)

ENTERPRISE NAME

DEPARTMENT USE ONLY

SECTION 14 – PREDECESSOR/SUCCESSOR INFORMATION

COMPLETE THIS SECTION IF THE REGISTERING ENTERPRISE IS WHOLLY OR PARTIALLY SUCCEEDING A PREDECESSOR.
FOR ASSISTANCE, CONTACT THE NEAREST DEPARTMENT OF LABOR & INDUSTRY FIELD ACCOUNTING SERVICE OFFICE.

IF THE ENTERPRISE HAS MORE THAN ONE PREDECESSOR, PHOTOCOPY THIS PAGE TO PROVIDE THE FOLLOWING INFORMATION ABOUT EACH.

1. PREDECESSOR LEGAL NAME

2. PREDECESSOR PA UC ACCOUNT NUMBER

3. PREDECESSOR TRADE NAME

4. PREDECESSOR FEDERAL EIN

5. PREDECESSOR STREET ADDRESS | CITY/TOWN | STATE | ZIP CODE + 4

6. SPECIFY HOW THE BUSINESS WAS ACQUIRED:
☐ PURCHASE   ☐ CHANGE IN LEGAL STRUCTURE
☐ CONSOLIDATION   ☐ GIFT   ☐ MERGER   ☐ IRC SEC. 338 ELECTION   ☐ OTHER (SPECIFY) _____

7. ☐ ACQUISITION DATE _____

8. PERCENTAGE OF THE PREDECESSOR'S TOTAL BUSINESS (PA AND NON-PA) ACQUIRED _____ %

9. PERCENTAGE OF THE PREDECESSOR'S PA BUSINESS ACQUIRED _____ %
IF LESS THAN 100%, PROVIDE THE NAME(S) AND ADDRESS(ES) OF THE ESTABLISHMENT(S) THAT CONDUCTED OPERATIONS IN PA OR EMPLOYED PA RESIDENTS.
ATTACH ADDITIONAL 8 1/2 X 11 SHEETS IF NECESSARY.

NAME OF ESTABLISHMENT(S)   ADDRESS(ES)

10. WHAT WAS THE PREDECESSOR'S BUSINESS ACTIVITY IN THE PA BUSINESS THAT WAS ACQUIRED?

11. ASSETS ACQUIRED:
☐ ACCOUNTS RECEIVABLE   ☐ EQUIPMENT   ☐ LEASES   ☐ OTHER (SPECIFY)
☐ CONTRACTS   ☐ FIXTURES   ☐ MACHINERY
☐ CUSTOMERS/CLIENTS   ☐ FURNITURE   ☐ NAME AND/OR GOODWILL
☐ EMPLOYEES   ☐ INVENTORY   ☐ REAL ESTATE

12. ☐ YES   ☐ NO   HAS THE PREDECESSOR CEASED PAYING WAGES IN PA?   IF YES, ENTER THE DATE PA WAGES CEASED,
IF KNOWN. _____

13. ☐ YES   ☐ NO   HAS THE PREDECESSOR CEASED OPERATIONS IN PA?   IF YES, ENTER THE DATE PA OPERATIONS CEASED,
IF KNOWN. _____
IF NO, DESCRIBE THE PREDECESSOR'S PRESENT PA BUSINESS ACTIVITY, IF KNOWN _____

14. AT THE TIME OF TRANSFER FROM THE PREDECESSOR ENTERPRISE TO THE REGISTERING ENTERPRISE:

a. ☐ YES   ☐ NO   WERE ANY OF THE OWNERS, SHAREHOLDERS (5% OR GREATER), PARTNERS, OFFICERS, OR DIRECTORS OF THE PREDECESSOR
OR OF ANY AFFILIATE, SUBSIDIARY OR PARENT CORPORATION OF THE PREDECESSOR ALSO OWNERS, SHAREHOLDERS (5% OR
GREATER), PARTNERS, OFFICERS, OR DIRECTORS OF THE REGISTERING ENTERPRISE OR OF ANY AFFILIATE, SUBSIDIARY OR
PARENT CORPORATION OF THE REGISTERING ENTERPRISE?

b. ☐ YES   ☐ NO   WAS THE PREDECESSOR, OR ANY AFFILIATE, SUBSIDIARY OR PARENT CORPORATION OF THE PREDECESSOR, AN OWNER,
SHAREHOLDER (5% OR GREATER), OR PARTNER IN THE REGISTERING ENTERPRISE?

c. ☐ YES   ☐ NO   WAS THE REGISTERING ENTERPRISE, OR ANY AFFILIATE, SUBSIDIARY OR PARENT CORPORATION OF THE REGISTERING
ENTERPRISE, AN OWNER, SHAREHOLDER (5% OR GREATER), OR PARTNER IN THE PREDECESSOR?

IF THE ANSWER TO ANY OF THE QUESTIONS IN 14 IS YES, PROVIDE THE FOLLOWING INFORMATION. ATTACH ADDITIONAL 8 1/2 X 11 SHEETS IF NECESSARY.

* IDENTIFY THOSE PERSONS AND ENTITIES BY THEIR FULL NAME;

* DESCRIBE THEIR RELATIONSHIP TO THE PREDECESSOR AND ANY AFFILIATE, SUBSIDIARY AND PARENT CORPORATION OF THE PREDECESSOR; AND

* DESCRIBE THEIR RELATIONSHIP TO THE REGISTERING ENTERPRISE AND ANY AFFILIATE, SUBSIDIARY AND PARENT CORPORATION OF THE REGISTERING ENTERPRISE.

THE REGISTERING ENTERPRISE MAY APPLY FOR A TRANSFER IN WHOLE OR IN PART OF THE PREDECESSOR'S UNEMPLOYMENT COMPENSATION (UC)
EXPERIENCE RECORD AND RESERVE ACCOUNT BALANCE, IF THE REGISTERING ENTERPRISE IS CONTINUING ESSENTIALLY THE SAME BUSINESS
ACTIVITY AS THE PREDECESSOR AND BOTH PROVIDED PA COVERED EMPLOYMENT. COMPLETE SECTION 15 AND, IF APPLICABLE, SECTION 16.

NOTE: A REGISTERING ENTERPRISE MAY APPLY THE UC TAXABLE WAGES PAID BY A PREDECESSOR TOWARD THE REGISTERING ENTERPRISE'S UC TAXABLE WAGE BASE FOR THE CALENDAR YEAR OF
ACQUISITION WITHOUT TRANSFERRING THE PREDECESSOR'S EXPERIENCE RECORD AND RESERVE ACCOUNT BALANCE.

Pennsylvania – continued.

ENTERPRISE NAME	DEPARTMENT USE ONLY

SECTION 15 – APPLICATION FOR PA UC EXPERIENCE RECORD AND RESERVE ACCOUNT BALANCE OF PREDECESSOR

A REGISTERING ENTERPRISE MAY APPLY THE UNEMPLOYMENT COMPENSATION (UC) TAXABLE WAGES PAID BY A PREDECESSOR TOWARD THE REGISTERING ENTERPRISE'S UC TAXABLE WAGE BASE FOR THE CALENDAR YEAR OF ACQUISITION WITHOUT TRANSFERRING THE PREDECESSOR'S EXPERIENCE RECORD AND RESERVE ACCOUNT BALANCE.

REFER TO THE INSTRUCTIONS TO DETERMINE IF IT IS ADVANTAGEOUS TO APPLY FOR A PREDECESSOR'S UC EXPERIENCE RECORD AND RESERVE ACCOUNT BALANCE.

IMPORTANT: THIS APPLICATION CANNOT BE CONSIDERED UNLESS IT IS SIGNED BY AN AUTHORIZED SIGNATORY OF BOTH THE PREDECESSOR AND THE REGISTERING ENTERPRISE. THE TRANSFER IN WHOLE OR IN PART OF THE EXPERIENCE RECORD AND RESERVE ACCOUNT BALANCE IS BINDING AND IRREVOCABLE ONCE IT HAS BEEN APPROVED BY THE DEPARTMENT OF LABOR AND INDUSTRY.

APPLICATION IS HEREBY MADE BY THE PREDECESSOR AND THE REGISTERING ENTERPRISE FOR A TRANSFER TO THE REGISTERING ENTERPRISE OF THE PENNSYLVANIA UNEMPLOYMENT COMPENSATION EXPERIENCE RECORD AND RESERVE ACCOUNT BALANCE OF THE PREDECESSOR TO THE EXTENT OF THE TRANSFER.

Generally can skip this section

WE HEREBY CERTIFY THAT THE TRANSFER REFERENCED IN SECTION 14 HAS OCCURRED AS DESCRIBED THEREIN AND THAT THE REGISTERING ENTERPRISE IS CONTINUING ESSENTIALLY THE SAME BUSINESS ACTIVITY AS THE PREDECESSOR. WE ALSO HEREBY CERTIFY THAT THE TRANSFER REFERENCED IN SECTION 14 WAS NOT UNDERTAKEN PRIMARILY TO OBTAIN A LOWER UC TAX RATE, BUT HAD A LEGITIMATE BUSINESS PURPOSE UNRELATED TO UNEMPLOYMENT COMPENSATION TAXES.

COMPLETE THIS SECTION ONLY IF YOU WANT TO APPLY FOR THE PREDECESSOR'S EXPERIENCE RECORD AND RESERVE ACCOUNT BALANCE.

1. PREDECESSOR NAME		DATE
AUTHORIZED SIGNATURE	TYPE OR PRINT NAME	TITLE
2. REGISTERING ENTERPRISE NAME		DATE
AUTHORIZED SIGNATURE	TYPE OR PRINT NAME	TITLE

SECTION 16 – UNEMPLOYMENT COMPENSATION PARTIAL TRANSFER INFORMATION

COMPLETE THIS SECTION IF THE REGISTERING ENTERPRISE ACQUIRED ONLY PART OF THE PREDECESSORS PENNSYLVANIA (PA) BUSINESS AND IS MAKING APPLICATION FOR THE TRANSFER OF A PORTION OF THE PREDECESSORS EXPERIENCE RECORD AND RESERVE ACCOUNT BALANCE.

COMPLETE REPLACEMENT UC-2A FOR PARTIAL TRANSFER (FORM UC-252). THE PREDECESSOR'S PA PAYROLL RECORDS FOR THE TWO YEARS PRIOR TO THE QUARTER OF THE TRANSFER AND/OR ACQUISITION MUST REMAIN AVAILABLE TO THE REGISTERING ENTERPRISE TO ENABLE THE REGISTERING ENTERPRISE TO PROVIDE REQUIRED INFORMATION REGARDING SEPARATED AND/OR TRANSFERRED EMPLOYEES.

UNEMPLOYMENT COMPENSATION (UC) TAXABLE WAGES ARE THOSE WAGES THAT DO NOT EXCEED THE UC TAXABLE WAGE BASE APPLICABLE TO A GIVEN CALENDAR YEAR.

1. DATE WAGES FIRST PAID BY PREDECESSOR OR PRE-PREDECESSOR(S) IN THE PART OF THE PA BUSINESS OR WORKFORCE TRANSFERRED (ACQUIRED) FOR WHICH CONTRIBUTIONS WERE PAID UNDER THE PROVISIONS OF THE PA UC LAW. DATE:_____

2. ENTER THE NUMBER OF EMPLOYEES WHO WORKED IN THE PART OF THE BUSINESS OR WORKFORCE THAT WAS TRANSFERRED FOR EACH QUARTER IN THE TABLE BELOW. IF NO EMPLOYMENT WAS GIVEN IN ANY QUARTER, ENTER "0".

Generally can skip but if you employ PA residents you may be required to complete

YEAR____				YEAR____				YEAR____				YEAR____				YEAR____	
QUARTERS				QUARTERS				QUARTERS				QUARTERS				QUART	
1	2	3	4	1	2	3	4	1	2	3	4	1	2	3	4	1	2

3. ENTER THE NUMBER OF EMPLOYEES WHO WORKED IN THE ENTIRE BUSINESS FOR EACH QUARTER IN THE TABLE BELOW. IF NO EMPLOYMENT WAS GIVEN IN ANY QUARTER, ENTER "0".

YEAR____				YEAR____				YEAR____				YEAR____				YEAR____				YEAR____ OF TRANSFER			
QUARTERS				QUARTERS				QUARTERS				QUARTERS				QUARTERS				QUARTERS			
1	2	3	4	1	2	3	4	1	2	3	4	1	2	3	4	1	2	3	4	1	2	3	4

4. IF THE PART OF THE BUSINESS OR WORKFORCE THAT WAS TRANSFERRED WAS IN EXISTENCE FOR LESS THAN THREE FULL CALENDAR YEARS PRIOR TO THE YEAR OF TRANSFER, ENTER THE FOLLOWING:

   A. TOTAL NUMBER OF EMPLOYEES WHO EARNED TAXABLE WAGES IN THE PART OF THE BUSINESS OR WORKFORCE THAT WAS TRANSFERRED DURING THE PERIOD FROM THE FIRST DAY OF THE QUARTER OF TRANSFER TO THE DATE OF TRANSFER _____

   B. TOTAL NUMBER OF EMPLOYEES WHO EARNED TAXABLE WAGES IN THE ENTIRE BUSINESS DURING THE PERIOD FROM THE FIRST DAY OF THE QUARTER OF TRANSFER TO THE DATE OF TRANSFER _____

5. PREDECESSORS ENTIRE PA UC TAXABLE PAYROLL, FOR THE PERIOD FROM THE FIRST DAY OF THE QUARTER OF TRANSFER TO THE DATE OF TRANSFER _____

Pennsylvania – continued.

PA-100 (03-09)

ENTERPRISE NAME	DEPARTMENT USE ONLY

SECTION 17 – MULTIPLE ESTABLISHMENT INFORMATION

COMPLETE THIS SECTION FOR EACH ADDITIONAL ESTABLISHMENT CONDUCTING BUSINESS IN PA OR EMPLOYING PA RESIDENTS. PHOTOCOPY THIS SECTION AS NECESSARY.

PART 1 ESTABLISHMENT INFORMATION

1. ESTABLISHMENT NAME (doing business as)		2. DATE OF FIRST OPERATIONS	3. TELEPHONE NUMBER ( )
4. STREET ADDRESS	CITY/TOWN	COUNTY	STATE	ZIP CODE + 4
5. PA SCHOOL DISTRICT		6. PA MUNICIPALITY	

PART 2 ESTABLISHMENT BUSINESS ACTIVITY INFORMATION

Unless you live in PA you probably will not have multiple establishments

REFER TO THE INSTRUCTIONS ON PAGES 20 & 21 TO COMPLETE THIS SECTION.

1. ENTER THE PERCENTAGE EACH PA BUSINESS ACTIVITY REPRESENTS OF THE TOTAL RECEIPTS OR REVENUES AT THIS ESTABLISHMENT. LIST PRODUCTS OR SERVICES ASSOCIATED WITH EACH BUSINESS ACTIVITY AND THE PERCENTAGE REPRESENTING OF THE TOTAL RECEIPTS OR REVENUES.

PA BUSINESS ACTIVITY	%	PRODUCTS OR SERVICES	%	ADDITIONAL PRODUCTS OR SERVICES	%
Accommodation & Food Services					
Agriculture, Forestry, Fishing, & Hunting					
Art, Entertainment, & Recreation Services					
Communications/Information					
Construction (must complete question 3)					
Domestics (Private Households)					
Educational Services					
Finance					
Health Care Services					
Insurance					
Management, Support & Remediation Services					
Manufacturing					
Mining, Quarrying, & Oil/Gas Extraction					
Other Services					
Professional, Scientific, & Technical Services					
Public Administration					
Real Estate					
Retail Trade					
Sanitary Service					
Social Assistance Services					
Transportation					
Utilities					
Warehousing					
Wholesale Trade					
TOTAL	100%				

2. ENTER THE PERCENTAGE THAT THIS ESTABLISHMENT'S RECEIPTS OR REVENUES REPRESENT OF THE TOTAL PA RECEIPTS OR REVENUES OF THE ENTERPRISE _____ %

3. ESTABLISHMENTS ENGAGED IN CONSTRUCTION MUST ENTER THE PERCENTAGE OF CONSTRUCTION ACTIVITY THAT IS NEW AND/OR RENOVATIVE AND THE PERCENTAGE OF CONSTRUCTION ACTIVITY THAT IS RESIDENTIAL AND/OR COMMERCIAL.

_____ % NEW + _____ % RENOVATIVE = 100%

_____ % RESIDENTIAL + _____ % COMMERCIAL = 100%

Pennsylvania – continued.

PA-100 (03-09)

ENTERPRISE NAME

DEPARTMENT USE ONLY

PART 3 ESTABLISHMENT SALES INFORMATION

1. ☐ YES ☐ NO IS THIS ESTABLISHMENT SELLING TAXABLE PRODUCTS OR OFFERING TAXABLE SERVICES TO CONSUMERS FROM A LOCATION IN PENNSYLVANIA? IF YES, COMPLETE SECTION 18.

2. ☐ YES ☐ NO IS THIS ESTABLISHMENT SELLING CIGARETTES IN PENNSYLVANIA? IF YES, COMPLETE SECTIONS 18 AND 19.

3. LIST EACH COUNTY IN PENNSYLVANIA WHERE THIS ESTABLISHMENT IS CONDUCTING TAXABLE SALES ACTIVITY(IES).

COUNTY _____ COUNTY _____ COUNTY _____

COUNTY _____ COUNTY _____ COUNTY _____

ATTACH ADDITIONAL 8 1/2 X 11 SHEETS IF NECESSARY.

PART 4a ESTABLISHMENT EMPLOYMENT INFORMATION

1. ☐ YES ☐ NO DOES THIS ESTABLISHMENT EMPLOY INDIVIDUALS WHO WORK IN PENNSYLVANIA? IF YES, INDICATE:
   a. DATE WAGES FIRST PAID (MM/DD/YYYY) .... _____
   b. DATE WAGES RESUMED FOLLOWING A BREAK IN EMPLOYMENT .... _____
   c. TOTAL NUMBER OF EMPLOYEES .... _____
   d. NUMBER OF EMPLOYEES PRIMARILY WORKING IN NEW BUILDING OR INFRASTRUCTURE .... _____
   e. NUMBER OF EMPLOYEES PRIMARILY WORKING IN REMODELING CONSTRUCTION .... _____
   f. ESTIMATED GROSS WAGES PER QUARTER .... $ _____ .00

2. ☐ YES ☐ NO DOES THIS ESTABLISHMENT EMPLOY PA RESIDENTS WHO WORK OUTSIDE OF PENNSYLVANIA? IF YES, INDICATE:
   a. DATE WAGES FIRST PAID (MM/DD/YYYY) .... _____
   b. DATE WAGES RESUMED FOLLOWING A BREAK IN EMPLOYMENT .... _____
   c. ESTIMATED GROSS WAGES PER QUARTER .... $ _____ .00

3. ☐ YES ☐ NO DOES THIS ESTABLISHMENT PAY REMUNERATION FOR SERVICES TO PERSONS YOU DO NOT CONSIDER EMPLOYEES? IF YES, EXPLAIN THE SERVICES PERFORMED _____

PART 4b

1. ☐ YES ☐ NO IS THIS REGISTRATION A RESULT OF A TAXABLE DISTRIBUTION FROM A BENEFIT TRUST, DEFERRED PAYMENT OR RETIREMENT PLAN FOR PA RESIDENTS? IF YES, INDICATE:
   a. DATE BENEFITS FIRST PAID (MM/DD/YYYY) .... _____
   b. ESTIMATED BENEFITS PAID PER QUARTER .... $ _____ .00

SECTION 6A – ADDITIONAL OWNERS, PARTNERS, SHAREHOLDERS, OFFICERS, AND RESPONSIBLE PARTY INFORMATION

PROVIDE THE FOLLOWING FOR ALL INDIVIDUAL AND/OR ENTERPRISE OWNERS, PARTNERS, SHAREHOLDERS, OFFICERS, AND RESPONSIBLE PARTIES. IF STOCK IS PUBLICLY TRADED, PROVIDE THE FOLLOWING FOR ANY SHAREHOLDER WITH AN EQUITY POSITION OF 5% OR MORE. PHOTOCOPY IF ADDITIONAL SPACE IS NEEDED.

1. NAME		2. SOCIAL SECURITY NUMBER	3. DATE OF BIRTH *	4. FEDERAL EIN
5. ☐ OWNER ☐ OFFICER ☐ PARTNER ☐ SHAREHOLDER ☐ RESPONSIBLE PARTY	6. TITLE	7. EFFECTIVE DATE OF TITLE	8. PERCENTAGE OF OWNERSHIP %	9. EFFECTIVE DATE OF OWNERSHIP
10. HOME ADDRESS (street)	CITY/TOWN	COUNTY	STATE	ZIP CODE + 4

11. THIS PERSON IS RESPONSIBLE TO REMIT/MAINTAIN: ☐ SALES TAX ☐ EMPLOYER WITHHOLDING TAX ☐ MOTOR FUEL TAXES ☐ WORKERS' COMPENSATION COVERAGE

1. NAME		2. SOCIAL SECURITY NUMBER	3. DATE OF BIRTH *	4. FEDERAL EIN
5. ☐ OWNER ☐ OFFICER ☐ PARTNER ☐ SHAREHOLDER ☐ RESPONSIBLE PARTY	6. TITLE	7. EFFECTIVE DATE OF TITLE	8. PERCENTAGE OF OWNERSHIP %	9. EFFECTIVE DATE OF OWNERSHIP
10. HOME ADDRESS (street)	CITY/TOWN	COUNTY	STATE	ZIP CODE + 4

11. THIS PERSON IS RESPONSIBLE TO REMIT/MAINTAIN: ☐ SALES TAX ☐ EMPLOYER WITHHOLDING TAX ☐ MOTOR FUEL TAXES ☐ WORKERS' COMPENSATION COVERAGE

* DATE OF BIRTH REQUIRED ONLY IF APPLYING FOR A CIGARETTE WHOLESALE DEALER'S LICENSE, A SMALL GAMES OF CHANCE DISTRIBUTOR LICENSE, OR A SMALL GAMES OF CHANCE MANUFACTURER CERTIFICATE.

Please visit e-ComSalesTax.com for more information

Pennsylvania – continued.

ENTERPRISE NAME	DEPARTMENT USE ONLY

SECTION 18 – SALES USE AND HOTEL OCCUPANCY TAX LICENSE, PUBLIC TRANSPORTATION ASSISTANCE TAX LICENSE, VEHICLE RENTAL TAX, TRANSIENT VENDOR CERTIFICATE, PROMOTER LICENSE, OR WHOLESALER CERTIFICATE

PART 1 — SALES USE AND HOTEL OCCUPANCY TAX, PUBLIC TRANSPORTATION ASSISTANCE TAX, VEHICLE RENTAL TAX, OR WHOLESALER CERTIFICATE

ENTERPRISES APPLYING FOR A SALES, USE AND HOTEL OCCUPANCY TAX LICENSE, PUBLIC TRANSPORTATION ASSISTANCE TAX LICENSE, VEHICLE RENTAL TAX, AND/OR WHOLESALER CERTIFICATE.
COMPLETE PART 1. SALES TAX COLLECTED MUST BE SEGREGATED FROM OTHER FUNDS AND MUST REMAIN IN THE COMMONWEALTH OF PENNSYLVANIA UNTIL REMITTED TO THE DEPARTMENT OF REVENUE.

IF THE ENTERPRISE IS:

* SELLING TAXABLE PRODUCTS OR SERVICES TO CONSUMERS IN PENNSYLVANIA, ENTER DATE OF FIRST TAXABLE SALE _____
* PURCHASING TAXABLE PRODUCTS OR SERVICES FOR ITS OWN USE IN PENNSYLVANIA AND INCURRING NO SALES TAX, ENTER DATE OF FIRST PURCHASE _____
* SELLING NEW TIRES TO CONSUMERS IN PENNSYLVANIA, ENTER DATE OF FIRST SALE _____
* LEASING OR RENTING MOTOR VEHICLES, ENTER DATE OF FIRST LEASE OR RENTAL _____
* RENTING FIVE OR MORE MOTOR VEHICLES, ENTER DATE OF FIRST RENTAL _____
* CONDUCTING RETAIL SALES IN PENNSYLVANIA AND NOT MAINTAINING A PERMANENT LOCATION IN PA, ENTER DATE OF FIRST TAXABLE SALE _____ (COMPLETE PART 2)
* ACTIVELY PROMOTING SHOWS IN PENNSYLVANIA WHERE TAXABLE PRODUCTS WILL BE OFFERED FOR RETAIL SALE, ENTER DATE OF FIRST SHOW _____ (COMPLETE PART 3)   ← **Trade Shows**
* ENGAGED SOLELY IN THE SALE OF TANGIBLE PERSONAL PROPERTY AND/OR SERVICES FOR RESALE OR RENTAL, ENTER DATE OF FIRST PURCHASE _____

PART 2 — TRANSIENT VENDOR CERTIFICATE

IF THE ENTERPRISE PARTICIPATES IN ANY SHOWS OTHER THAN THOSE LISTED, PROVIDE THE NAME(S) OF THE SHOW(S) AND INFORMATION ABOUT THE SHOW(S) TO THE DEPARTMENT OF REVENUE AT LEAST 10 DAYS PRIOR TO THE SHOW.

PROVIDE THE FOLLOWING INFORMATION FOR EACH SHOW:

1. PROMOTER NUMBER	2. SHOW NAME	3. COUNTY	
4. SHOW ADDRESS (STREET, CITY, STATE, ZIP)		5. START DATE	6. END DATE
1. PROMOTER NUMBER	2. SHOW NAME	3. COUNTY	
4. SHOW ADDRESS (STREET, CITY, STATE, ZIP)		5. START DATE	6. END DATE

ATTACH ADDITIONAL 8 1/2 X 11 SHEETS IF NECESSARY.

PART 3 — PROMOTER LICENSE

PROVIDE THE FOLLOWING INFORMATION FOR EACH SHOW:

1. SHOW NAME	2. TYPE OF SHOW	3. START DATE	4. END DATE
5. SHOW ADDRESS (STREET, CITY, STATE, ZIP)		6. COUNTY	7. NBR OF VENDORS
1. SHOW NAME	2. TYPE OF SHOW	3. START DATE	4. END DATE
5. SHOW ADDRESS (STREET, CITY, STATE, ZIP)		6. COUNTY	7. NBR OF VENDORS

ATTACH ADDITIONAL 8 1/2 X 11 SHEETS IF NECESSARY.

The rest of the pages in the PA app can generally be ignored unless you are selling products in one of the specific areas covered by those pages. Also, the tax-exempt section is not referring to retail sales and can also be skipped.

SOUTH CAROLINA DEPARTMENT OF REVENUE
TAX REGISTRATION APPLICATION

INTERNET REGISTRATION: SCBOS.SC.GOV

Mail TO: SC DEPARTMENT OF REVENUE
REGISTRATION UNIT
COLUMBIA, SC 29214-0140

Please Print
Use Blue or
Black Ink

SID# _____
W/H _____
SALES _____
USE _____
PARTNERSHIP _____
LICENSE TAX _____

SCDOR-111
(Rev. 12/20/11)
8048

Section A: Taxes to be Registered for This Business Location - Make Checks Payable to SCDOR

☐ Retail Sales/Accommodations License ($50 license tax is required)   ☐ Artist & Craftsman's License ($20 license tax is required)
☐ Withholding Tax (Page 2) ☐ Nonresident Withholding Exemption (Page 2) ☐ Use Tax (No fee required)

1. Owner, Partnership, or Corporate Charter Name
ABC Toys, LLC

2. FEIN _____
SSN _____

3. Mailing Address (for all correspondence)

_____
In Care Of

_____
Street

_____
City   State   ZIP

4. Type of Ownership
☐ Sole Proprietor (one owner)
☐ Partnership (two or more owners, other than LLP)
☐ LLC/LLP filing as:
   ☐ Corporation ☐ Partnership ☐ Single Member
☐ South Carolina Corporation
   Date Incorporated _____
☐ Foreign Corporation
   State and Date Incorporated _____
☐ Other (explain) _____

5. Business Phone Number

6. Daytime Phone Number

7. Email Address

8. Fax Number

9. Physical Location of Business (No P.O. Box)
Required For All Tax Types

_____
Street

_____
City   County (Required)   State   ZIP

10. Is Physical Location within S.C. City Limits?

☐ Yes ☐ No ← Generally no, unless you live in SC

Which city? _____

Section B: Retail Sales/Accommodations/Artist & Craftsman License/Use Tax

In and out-of-state sellers. A retail license will not be issued to a person with any outstanding state tax liability.

11. How Would You Like to File? ☐ Monthly ☐ Quarterly (See Instructions)

12. Is Your Business Seasonal? ☐ Yes ☐ No If yes, list months active: _____

You must file a zero return for periods with no sales. See Instructions for Filing Guidelines

Will get reviewed by DOR periodically and your status could be changed

13. How Many Retail Sales Locations Do You Operate in S.C. under Your Ownership? _____

14. Trade Name (Doing Business As)

15. Location of Records (No P.O. Box)

16. Main Business (i.e., Retail Sales, Manufacturing, Service, etc.)
Retail sales conducted online

17. Anticipated Date of First Retail Sales
mm/dd/yy

18. Type of Business

☐ Agriculture, Forestry, Fishing, & Hunting (11)
☐ Mining (21)
☐ Utilities (22)
☐ Construction (23)
☐ Manufacturing (31-33)
☐ Wholesale Trade (42)
☐ Durable Medical Equipment (44)

☐ Max Tax (Vehicles) (44)
☐ Retail Trade (44-45)
☐ Artists & Craftsman (45)
☐ Transportation & Warehouse (48-49)
☐ Information (51)
☐ Finance & Insurance (52)
☐ Real Estate, Rental & Leasing (53)

☐ Professional, Scientific, & Technical Services (54)
☐ Management of Companies & Enterprises (55)
☐ Administrative & Support, Waste Management & Remediation Services (56)
☐ Education Services (61)

☐ Health Care & Social Assistance (62)
☐ Arts, Entertainment, & Recreation (71)
☐ Accommodation & Food Services (72)
☐ Other Services (81)
☐ Public Administration (92)

19. Check If You Sell These Products

☐ Motor Oil   ☐ Tires   ☐ Lead Acid Batteries   ☐ Large Appliances   ☐ Aviation Gasoline/Jet Fuel
☐ Prepaid Wireless Cards   ☐ Service to Cellular and Personal Communications Users

---

Please visit e-ComSalesTax.com for more information

South Carolina – continued.

Unless you live in SC or have employees in SC, you do not need to complete this section

Section C: Withholding Tax

Every employer having employees earning wages in SC must register for withholding. Other types of payments also require state tax withholding. See instructions for more information.

20. Check the box that applies to your business:

☐ 02 **Resident business**: Principal place of business is inside South Carolina.

☐ 05 **Nonresident Business**: Principal place of business is outside of South Carolina.

21. Filing Frequency:

☐ **Quarterly**: Returns must be filed every quarter.

☐ 01 **Annual**: All employees are household employees, farmers, fishermen or ministers. Returns are filed at the end of each calendar year.

22. Anticipated Date of First Payroll (mm/dd/yyyy): _____

This date will be used as the open date of your withholding account, and returns must be filed beginning with this date regardless of activity.

Section D: Nonresident Withholding Exemption

Check the appropriate block to administratively register with the Department and claim exemption from nonresident withholding required by SC Code Sections 12-8-540 (rents and royalties), 12-8-550 (temporarily doing business or performing services in SC), or 12-8-570 (trust or estate beneficiaries). The exempt person agrees to be subject to the jurisdiction of the Department and the S.C. courts to determine S.C. tax liability, including withholding, estimated taxes, and interest and penalties, if any. Registering is not an admission of tax liability, and, does not, by itself, require the filing of a tax return.

See instructions for further information.

☐ I agree to file SC tax return   ☐ I am not subject to SC Tax Jurisdiction (no NEXUS)

Section E: Name(s) of Business Owner, General Partners, Officers, or Members

Social Security Number	Name/Title/General Partners	Home Address

Social Security Privacy Act

It is mandatory that you provide your social security number on this tax form. 42 U.S.C 405(c)(2)(C)(i) permits a state to use an individual's social security number as means of identification in administration of any tax. SC Regulation 117-1 mandates that any person required to make a return to the SC Department of Revenue shall provide identifying numbers, as prescribed, for securing proper identification. Your social security number is used for identification purposes.

Upon completion of **both pages, sign and date the application below.**

I certify that all information on this application, including any attachments, is true and correct to the best of my knowledge.

_____   _____   _____
SIGNATURE OF OWNER, ALL PARTNERS, OR CORPORATE OFFICER   TITLE   DATE

MAIL TO: SC DEPARTMENT OF REVENUE
REGISTRATION UNIT
COLUMBIA, SOUTH CAROLINA 29214-0140
If you have questions about this form, please call (803) 896-1350.

Please visit e-ComSalesTax.com for more information

TENNESSEE DEPARTMENT OF REVENUE
APPLICATION FOR REGISTRATION

ANSWER ALL QUESTIONS COMPLETELY. INCOMPLETE AND UNSIGNED APPLICATIONS WILL DELAY PROCESSING. FOR ASSISTANCE YOU MAY CONTACT ANY OF THE TAXPAYER AND VEHICLE SERVICES OFFICES LISTED ON THE BACK.

1. CHECK ANY OF THE FOLLOWING TAX, PERMIT, OR FEE REQUIREMENTS FOR WHICH YOUR BUSINESS IS LIABLE:

*ALCOHOLIC BEVERAGE TAXES:
____ Beer Barrelage
____ Brand Registration
____ Liquor By The Drink
____ Wholesale Beer
____ Wholesale Gallonage
____ Winery Tax

**BUSINESS TAX
____ Classification 1
____ Classification 2
____ Classification 3
____ Classification 4
____ Classification 5

GROSS RECEIPTS TAXES:
____ Bottlers
____ Mixing Bar
____ Gas, Water, Electric Power & Light

____ FRANCHISE AND EXCISE TAXES
____ Series LLC (See Instructions)

PRIVILEGE TAXES:
____ Auto Rental Surcharge
____ Bail Bondsmen
____ Litigation Tax
____ Professional Privilege Tax

____ ***PETROLEUM TAXES**

____ SALES AND USE TAX

SEVERANCE TAXES:
____ Coal
____ Crude Oil/Natural Gas
____ Mineral

SOLID WASTE TAXES:
____ Tire
____ Used Oil

____ TOBACCO TAX

____ WINE DIRECT SHIPPER

> Generally the answer is yes to first two

*Requires Bond. **TYPE OF BOND:** ☐ 1. SURETY ☐ 2. CASH ☐ 3. CERTIFICATE

**The local county clerk and designated municipal business tax official in your area also have business tax registra...

2. REASON FOR APPLYING:
☐ 1. New business
☐ 2. Additional location
☐ 3. Purchase of existing business

3. WILL YOUR GROSS SALES EXCEED $4,800 PER YEAR? ☐ YES ☐ NO
WILL YOUR TAXABLE SERVICES EXCEED $1,200 PER YEAR? ☐ YES ☐ NO
DO YOU HAVE SUPPLIERS (IN-STATE OR OUT-OF-STATE) WHO DO NOT COLLECT TN. SALES TAX? ☐ YES ☐ NO
IF ALL THREE OF THE ABOVE ARE "NO", YOU DO NOT NEED A SALES TAX #.

4a. DATE BUSINESS BEGAN IN TENNESSEE AT THIS LOCATION _____

4b. FISCAL YR. END _____ / _____
MO / DAY

5. WILL YOU BE COLLECTING OVER $200 PER MONTH IN SALES TAX?
☐ YES ☐ NO

6. HOW MANY MONTHS OF THE YEAR WILL YOU HAVE SALES AND/OR USE TAX TO REPORT?
_____

7. BUSINESS NAME AND EXACT LOCATION
BUSINESS NAME (ATTACH LIST IF NECESSARY FOR ADDITIONAL LOCATIONS)

STREET, HIGHWAY (DO NOT USE P.O. BOX NUMBER OR RURAL ROUTE NUMBER)

CITY   STATE   ZIP CODE   COUNTY

8. BUSINESS MAILING ADDRESS
NAME (ENTER CORPORATION NAME, IF APPLICABLE)

> Depends on your business

P.O. BOX, STREET, ROU...

CITY   STATE   ZIP CODE

9. IS THIS BUSINESS LOCATED INSIDE ANY TENNESSEE CITY LIMITS? ☐ YES ☐ NO
IF YES, WHAT CITY? _____

10. RECORD STORAGE ADDRESS:
STREET, HIGHWAY (DO NOT USE P.O. BOX NUMBER)
CITY   STATE   ZIP CODE

11. BUSINESS TELEPHONE #
( )
AREA CODE
FAX #

12. ENTER YOUR FEDERAL EMPLOYER'S IDENTIFICATION # [ ][ ] — [ ][ ][ ][ ][ ][ ]
☐ APPLIED FOR
☐ NOT REQUIRED

13a. BUSINESS CONTACT PERSON:

13b. E-MAIL ADDRESS:

14. TYPE OF OWNERSHIP:
☐ PROPRIETORSHIP ☐ HUSBAND/WIFE OWNERSHIP ☐ PARTNERSHIP ☐ LIMITED PARTNERSHIP
☐ LIMITED LIABILITY COMPANY ☐ PROFESSIONAL LIMITED LIABILITY COMPANY
☐ CORPORATION ☐ S CORPORATION ☐ PROFESSIONAL CORPORATION ☐ OTHER

NAME OF CORPORATION _____ SEC. OF STATE # _____

15. CURRENT OR PRIOR TAX NUMBER (SALES TAX, ETC.)

_____ / _____
TAX TYPE   ACCOUNT NO.

16. DESCRIBE THE BUSINESS ACTIVITY AT THIS LOCATION, STATING THE MAJOR PRODUCTS AND/OR SERVICES SOLD.
Online retail sales of books, games, toys, tools, etc. to end users

A. Are your sales 100% over-the-counter sales? _____ Yes _____ No
(Note: If you _ever_ have a sale for which you ship or deliver merchandise, do not check "Yes.")

B. If not 100% over-the-counter sales, how many cities or counties in Tennessee, other than the location of your business do you ship or deliver merchandise to in an average month? _____

> Generally no science to this, just an estimate will do

RV-F1300501

Tennessee – continued.

C. Do you use/have access to: (a) Automated systems _____ Yes (b) Computers _____ Yes (c) Internet _____ Yes?

D. Do you lease tangible personal property in one location for use in another? _____ Yes _____ No

E. Do you lease space in a business location to another company? _____ Yes _____ No

F. Do you sell at retail? _____ Yes _____ No Wholesale? _____ Yes _____ No Both? _____ Yes _____ No

G. If you are a contractor, do you perform contracts in the city or county where your business is located? _____ Yes _____ No

H. If you are a contractor, do you perform contracts in a city or county where your business is not located? _____ Yes _____ No

I. If you are a contractor, do you install everything you sell? _____ Yes _____ No

---

17. EDI/EFT DO YOU CURRENTLY FILE YOUR RETURN BY EDI? ☐ YES ☐ NO DO YOU CURRENTLY REMIT PAYMENT BY EFT? ☐ YES ☐ NO

WOULD YOU LIKE TO RECEIVE INFORMATION ABOUT THE FOLLOWING: ☐ EDI ☐ EFT

18. IDENTIFY OWNERS, OFFICERS, MEMBERS, OR PARTNERS (ATTACH ADDITIONAL NAMES ON SEPARATE SHEET).

(1) NAME	HOME TELEPHONE #	☐ SOCIAL SECURITY #	☐ FEDERAL EIN
HOME ADDRESS (DO NOT USE P.O. BOX #)	CITY	STATE	ZIP CODE

☐ Member ☐ Officer ☐ Partner ☐ Owner - Individual ☐ Owner - Company

(2) NAME	HOME TELEPHONE #	☐ SOCIAL SECURITY #	☐ FEDERAL EIN
HOME ADDRESS (DO NOT USE P.O. BOX #)	CITY	STATE	ZIP CODE

☐ Member ☐ Officer ☐ Partner ☐ Owner - Individual ☐ Owner - Company

(3) NAME	HOME TELEPHONE #	☐ SOCIAL SECURITY #	☐ FEDERAL EIN
HOME ADDRESS (DO NOT USE P.O. BOX #)	CITY	STATE	ZIP CODE

☐ Member ☐ Officer ☐ Partner ☐ Owner - Individual ☐ Owner - Company

PREVIOUS BUSINESS NAME	PREVIOUS OWNER'S TELEPHONE # ( )	STILL IN BUSINESS? ☐ YES ☐ NO
PREVIOUS OWNER'S NAME AND ADDRESS		

---

19. IF YOU ARE AN OUT-OF-STATE BUSINESS THAT WILL BE DOING BUSINESS IN TENNESSEE, PLEASE ANSWER THE FOLLOWING QUESTION.

DO YOU HAVE A LOCATION OR OFFICE IN TENNESSEE? ☐ YES ☐ NO IF YES, NAME LOCATION:

20. THE STATEMENTS MADE ON THIS APPLICATION ARE TRUE TO THE BEST OF MY KNOWLEDGE AND BELIEF. (THIS APPLICATION MUST BE SIGNED BY THE INDIVIDUAL OWNER, A PARTNER, OR AN OFFICER OF THE CORPORATION LISTED IN ITEM 17.)

FOR DEPARTMENT USE ONLY

SIGN HERE: _____

OWNER, PARTNER, OR OFFICER (DO NOT PRINT OR USE STAMP)

> Answer should include "own inventory in Tennessee"

For additional information, contact the Taxpayer and Vehicle Services Division in one of our Department of Revenue Offices:

Chattanooga	Jackson	Johnson City	Knoxville	Memphis	Nashville
(423) 634-6266	(731) 423-5747	(423) 854-5321	(865) 594-6100	(901) 213-1400	(615) 253-0600
Suite 350	Suite 340	204 High Point Drive	Room 606	3150 Appling Road	3rd Floor
State Office Building	Lowell Thomas Building	PO Box 2365	State Office Building	Bartlett, TN 38133	Andrew Jackson Building
540 McCallie Avenue	225 Martin Luther King Blvd.	Johnson City, TN 37605-2365	531 Henley Street		500 Deaderick Street
Chattanooga, TN 37402	Jackson, TN 38301		Knoxville, TN 37901		Nashville, TN 37242

Tennessee residents can also call our statewide toll free number at 1-800-342-1003. Out-of-state callers must dial (615) 253-0600.

Please visit e-ComSalesTax.com for more information

Form R-1

Virginia Department of Taxation
Business Registration Application

You can register a new business online using VATAX Online Services for Businesses at www.tax.virginia.gov
- Please read instructions carefully before completing this form.
- For assistance with this form or for information about taxes not listed in this form, call 804-367-8057.
- Completed form can either be mailed or faxed to: **Registration Unit Virginia Department of Taxation**
  P. O. Box 1114
  Richmond, VA 23218-1114
  FAX Number (804) 367-2603

Reason For Submitting this Form

Check One

☐ **New Business - Never Registered**
Complete Sections I through V.

☐ **Add Tax Types to Existing Registration**
Complete Sections I, II and V; also update Sections III and IV, if changed.

☐ **Add Additional Locations to Existing Registration**
Complete Sections I, II and V; also update Sections III and IV, if changed.

Section I - Business Information

1 Entity Type - Check One (See instructions)

☐ C Corporation
☐ S Corporation
☐ General Partnership
☐ Limited Partnership
☐ Limited Liability Partnership (LLP)

☐ Limited Liability Co. (LLC)
☐ Sole Proprietor
☐ Non-Profit Organization
☐ Non-Profit Corporation
☐ Estate/Trust

☐ Virginia State Government
☐ Federal Government
☐ Local Government
☐ Other State Gov't (not VA)
☐ Other Government

☐ Public Service Corporation
☐ Bank
☐ Savings and Loan
☐ Credit Union
☐ Cooperative

2 Business Name - Enter full legal name of business. Sole proprietors, enter owner's name (first, middle initial, last).

3 Taxpayer Identification Number

a) FEIN - Enter your Federal Employer Identification Number (FEIN). All businesses obtain a FEIN at www.irs.gov.

b) SSN - If you are a Sole Proprietor and are not registering for employer withholding, enter your Social Security Number (SSN).

4 Principal Business Activity - Enter the description and code for your business (see instructions).

Description | Code

Physical and Mailing address can and most times are the same, even for out of state vendors

5 Primary Mailing Address
Street Address or PO Box

6 Primary Physical Address
Street Address | City, State and Zip Code

7 Business Formation - If a corporation, enter the state and the date of its incorporation. All others, enter the state and date of formation.
Incorporation or Formation State | Date of Incorporation or Formation (mm, dd, yyyy)

If LLC same applies

8 Contact Information - Enter business contact information for all your business entities.
Contact Person | Contact Phone Number (Including Area Code)

Email Address | FAX Number (Including Area Code)

Va.Dept. of Taxation R-1 1190 5220 (Rev 10/11)

Please visit e-ComSalesTax.com for more information

Virginia – continued.

Complete at the top of each page

FEIN at top of each page also

Business Name | Taxpayer Identification Number

Section II - Tax Types

A   Sales and Use Tax - Use this area to register for Sales and Use Taxes. See Instructions.

☐ Check this box if you do not need tax forms mailed to you. (You can file and pay your taxes online. See instructions.)

1 Filing Options - For businesses with multiple locations, indicate below how you want to submit your return(s).

☐ a. File one combined return for all business locations in the same locality.

no action if only one location

☐ b. File one consolidated return for all business locations. (See Instructions.)

☐ c. File a separate return for each business location.

2 Business Locations - Complete for each location. Photocopy this page if you have additional locations.

a) Add This Location to This Virginia Account Number

b) Trade Name of Business   c) Business Locality Code

d) Business Physical Street Address - If different from one shown on page 1. (No PO Boxes.)   City, State and ZIP

e) Contact Name - If different from one shown on page 1.   Contact Phone Number (Including Area Code)   Contact Email

f) Mailing Address - If different from above.

This is what VA calls sales tax for vendors who do not have a VA location. It is still tax you collect from customer

g) Principal Business Activity Code   Description of   Date Location Opened

i) Indicate Tax Type(s) & Beginning Liability Date For This Location You may be required to register for Litter Tax in Section F.

Each Tax Type Must Be Reported and Remitted Separately on the Appropriate Form

Tax Type	Date You Became Liable	Form Used to File and Pay Taxes
☐ Retail Sales Tax (In-State Dealers)	Date _____	File and Pay Using Form ST-9
☐ Use Tax (Out-of-State Dealers)	Date _____	File and Pay Using Form ST-8
☐ Consumer Use Tax	Date _____	File and Pay Using Form ST-7
☐ Motor Vehicle Wholesale Fuel Sales Tax	Date _____	File and Pay Using Form DFT-1
☐ Watercraft Tax	Date _____	File and Pay Using Form WCT-2
☐ Tire Recycling Fee	Date _____	File and Pay Using Form T-1
☐ Digital Media Fee	Date _____	File and Pay Using Form DM-1
☐ Aircraft Tax	Date _____	File and Pay Using Form AST-2

Number of Aircraft Owned Previous Year: _____

Virginia Commercial Fleet Aircraft License Number: _____

j) Seasonal Business - Check months business is active. (Complete if you are only open part of the year.)	JAN	FEB	MAR	APR	MAY	JUN	JUL	AUG	SEP	OCT	NOV	DEC

k) ☐ **Specialty Dealer** - Check this box if you sell at flea markets, craft shows, etc. at various locations in Virginia.

Virginia – continued.

Generally you can skip this section

Business Name		Taxpayer Identification Number

B Vending Machine Sales Tax

For Existing Accounts, Enter Virginia Account Number	Date You Became Liable for Vending Machine Tax

1 City or County and Locality Code - Enter each locality you will operate vending machines (see instructions).

	Locality 1	Locality 2	Locality 3	Locality 4	Locality 5	Locality 6
City or County						
Locality Code						

Unless you have employees in VA, you can skip

C Withholding Tax

For Existing Accounts, Enter Virginia Account Number	Date You Became Liable for Withholding Tax

☐ Check this box if you do not need tax forms mailed to you. (You can file and pay your taxes online. See instructions.)

1 Filing Frequency - Will be determined by the Dept. of Taxation and revieonly for withholding tax amount of Virginia Income Tax you expect to withhold each quarter.

☐ Quarterly Filer - Less Than $300 Virginia Withholding Per Quarter   ☐ Pension Plan Only

☐ Monthly Filer - Between $300 and $3,000 Virginia Withholding Per Quarter   ☐ Household Employer - Annual Filer - Total Household Payroll Not More Than $5,000 Per Quarter

☐ Semi-Weekly Filer - $3,000 or Greater Virginia Withholding Per Quarter

2 Seasonal Business - Check months business is active. (Complete if you are only open part of the year.)	JAN	FEB	MAR	APR	MAY	JUN	JUL	AUG	SEP	OCT	NOV	DEC

3 Mailing Address - If different from one shown on page 1.

Street Address or PO Box	City, State, ZIP

4 Contact Information - If different from one shown on page 1.

Name		Email Address

Depending upon your entity type you may not need to complete this section, please read instructions

D Corporation Income Tax

For Existing Accounts, Enter Virginia Account Number	

1 Tax Year - Must be same as your Federal taxable year. Check one.

☐ Calendar Year Filer (1/1 - 12/31)   OR   ☐ Fiscal Year Filer (Enter fiscal beginning and ending months.)

Beginning _____ Ending _____)

2 Contact Information

Name	Contact Phone Number (Including Area Code)	Email Address

3 Mailing Address - If different from one shown on page 1.

Street Address or PO Box	City, State, ZIP

4 Subsidiary or Affiliate - Complete the following only if this business is a subsidiary or affiliated with another business and the parent is filing a combined or consolidated return.

☐ Combined return. Check if business is a subsidiary or affiliate and parent files combined return.
☐ Consolidated return. Check if business is a subsidiary or affiliate and parent files consolidated return.

Parent Company's Business Name	Parent Company's FEIN

E Pass-Through Entity

For Existing Accounts, Enter Virginia Account Number	Date of Formation

1 Tax Year - Must be same as your Federal taxable year. Check one.

☐ Calendar Year Filer (1/1 - 12/31)   OR   ☐ Fiscal Year Filer (Enter fiscal beginning and ending months.)

Beginning _____ Ending _____)

2 Contact Information

Name	Contact Phone Number (Including Area Code)	Email Address

3 Mailing Address - If different from one shown on page 1.

Street Address or PO Box	City, State, ZIP

Please visit e-ComSalesTax.com for more information

Virginia – continued.

Generally you can skip this section

Business Name		Taxpayer Identification Number

F Miscellaneous Taxes

Tax Type - See instructions. Indicate tax type and the date you became liable.

☐ Corn Assessment   Date _____   ☐ Forest Products Tax Date _____   ☐ Small Grains Assessment   Date _____

☐ Cotton Assessment Date _____   ☐ Litter Tax   Date _____   ☐ Soft Drink Excise Tax   Date _____

☐ Egg Excise Tax   Date _____   ☐ Peanut Excise Tax   Date _____   ☐ Soybean Assessment   Date _____

☐ Sheep Assessment Date _____

G Communications Taxes

Generally you can skip this section

Date You Became Liable for Communications Taxes (Enter the _____ these taxes.)

1 **Communication Tax Type** - See instructions.
Indicate below the service/fee/tax type and the date that this service/fee/tax began (ADD) or Terminated (TERM).

ADD TERM

☐ ☐ Landline Telephone Service Date _____   ☐ ☐ Satellite Radio Service   Date _____

☐ ☐ Wireless Telephone Service Date _____   ☐ ☐ Other Communications Services   Date _____

☐ ☐ Cable Television Service   Date _____   ☐ ☐ Landline E-911 Tax   Date _____

☐ ☐ Satellite Television Service Date _____   ☐ ☐ Cable Public Rights-of-Way Use Fee Date _____

2 Were cable franchise agreements in force as of 1/1/07? ☐ Yes ☐ No (If Yes, attach Form CT-1. See instructions.)

3 Contact Name | Contact Phone Number (Including Area Code) | Email Address

Section III - Responsible Party

Under Section 58.1-1813 of the Code of Virginia, any corporate, partnership or limited liability officer may be held personally liable for unpaid taxes assessed against a corporation or partnership. This section must be comp... ...ability officer" as defined below.
The term "corporate, partnership or limited liability officer" includes any ... ...er, manager or employee of a partnership or limited liability company, who is under a duty to collect, ad... ...wledge of the failure to pay the tax, and who had the authority to prevent the failure. Attach additional p... ...in writing and include changes in names, addresses and telephone numbers.

As with most states, a responsible party will be required

Notify the Department of Taxation when there is a change of responsible parties.

	a) Name of Responsible Party		b) SSN	
1	c) Relationship Title	d) Relationship Date	e) Home Phone Number (Including Area Code)	f) Email Address
	g) Residence Address		h) City, State, ZIP	
	a) Name of Responsible Party		b) SSN	
2	c) Relationship Title	d) Relationship Date	e) Home Phone Number (Including Area Code)	f) Email Address
	g) Residence Address		h) City, State, ZIP	
	a) Name of Responsible Party		b) SSN	
3	c) Relationship Title	d) Relationship Date	e) Home Phone Number (Including Area Code)	f) Email Address
	g) Residence Address		h) City, State, ZIP	

Section IV - Electronic Funds Transfer (EFT)

Businesses with an average monthly Virginia employer withholding, sales and use, or corporation income tax liability exceeding $20,000 are required by law to pay that tax by Electronic Funds Transfer (EFT). This threshold applies to each tax separately. Check the box for each tax that EFT is required.

☐ Sales & Use Tax (In-State Dealers) ☐ Use Tax (Out-Of-State Dealers) ☐ Corporation Income Tax ☐ Employer Withholding Tax

Download the EFT guide at www.tax.virginia.gov

Section V - Signature

Important - Read Before Signing

This registration form must be signed by an officer of the corporation, limited liability company or unincorporated association, who is authorized to sign on behalf of the organization. The proprietor must sign for a sole proprietorship.

Under penalty of law, I believe the information on the application to be true and correct.

Signature		Title
Name Printed	Date	Daytime Phone Number (Including Area Code)

Page 4

Legal Entity/Owner Name

Unified Business Identifier (UBI)

Federal Employer Identification Number (FEIN)

For Validation - Office Use Only

03N-400-925-0003

Business License Application

For faster service - Apply online at business.wa.gov/BLS
or print in dark ink and mail to Business Licensing Service

1. Purpose of Application

Please check all boxes that apply.

☐ Open/Reopen Business
complete sections 2, 3, 4, (5 if hiring employees) and 6

☐ Open Additional Location
complete sections 2, 3, 4, (5 if hiring employees) and 6

☐ Change Ownership
complete sections 2, 3, 4, (5 if you have employees) and 6

☐ Register Trade Name
complete sections 2, 3, 4 and 6

☐ Change Trade Name - *complete sections 2, 3, 4 and 6*

Name(s) to be **cancelled**: _____

☐ Change Location - *complete sections 2, 3, 4 and 6*

Old address to be closed: _____

☐ Add License/Registration to Existing Location
complete sections 2, 3, 4, and 6

☐ Business Has or Will Have Employees
complete all sections

☐ Business Has or Will Have Employees Under Age 18
complete all sections

☐ Hire Persons to Work In or Around Your Home
complete all sections

☐ Other - *complete all sections* _____

2. Licenses and Fees

Use the License Fee Sheet for the information needed to complete this list.

Mark Registrations Needed:	Fees Due
☐ Tax Registration (State Dept. of Revenue) – Do you want a separate tax return for each business? ☐ Yes ☐ No	No Fee
☐ Industrial Insurance (Workers' Compensation) – *Required if you will have employees.*	No Fee
☐ Unemployment Insurance – *Required if you will have employees.*	No Fee
☐ Minor Work Permit – *Required if you will have employees under age 18.*	No Fee
☐ New Trade Name (Doing Business As): _____	$5.00

List Additional Trade Names *($5 each name)* **or Other Licenses** *(such as Lottery Retailer):*

➢	$
➢	$
➢	$
➢	$
➢	$
➢	$

Enclose check for **total amount due**, including the Processing Fee, which MUST be submitted with this form.

Make check payable to the Department of Revenue.

Processing Fee	$ 15.00
Total Amount Due	$

Please visit e-ComSalesTax.com for more information

Washington – continued.

3. Owner Information

a. *Select only ONE ownership structure:*

☐ Sole Proprietor
If married, should spouse's name appear on license? ☐ Yes ☐ No *(If you answer No, you must still enter the spouse information in section "3" below.)*

☐ Corporation* ☐ Non Profit Corporation* *(educational, religious, charitable)* ☐ Limited Liability Company*
☐ Partnership (# of partners:_____) ☐ Joint Venture
☐ Limited Partnership* ☐ Limited Liability Partnership* ☐ Limited Liability Limited Partnership*
These ownership structures must contact the Secretary of State office for additional filing requirements.

Name of Corporation, LLC, Partnership, LLP, LLLP, or Joint Venture Name (examples: ABC, Inc. OR Fir Trees Unlimited LLC)

State incorporated/formed: _____ ▼   Year incorporated/formed: _____

☐ Association ☐ Trust ☐ Municipality ☐ Tribal Government ☐ Other _____

Name of Organization (example: Anderson Family Trust)

b. Business Open Date _____ / _____   *Provide the ownership structure's first date of business at this location. Out-of-state businesses should use the first date of operation in WA. (Required. If unknown, please estimate.)*
MM   YY

c. _____   Is this location inside city limits? ☐ Yes ☐ No
Business Name/Trade Name

d. _____   _____
Business Mailing Address (Street or PO Box, Suite No. do not use building name)   Business Street Address (if different than mailing) Do not use a PO Box or PMB

_____   _____
City   State   Zip code   City   State   Zip code

e. (____) _____   (____) _____   _____
Business Telephone Number   Fax Number   E-Mail Address

f. *List all owners & spouses: Sole proprietor, partners, officers, or LLC members. (Attach additional pages if needed.)*

➢ _____   ____ / ____ _____ _____
Name (Last, First, Middle)   Date of Birth   Social Security Number*   % Owned

_____   _____
Home Address (Street or PO Box)   City   State   Zip code

_____   Are you married? ☐ Yes ☐ No If yes, enter spouse information below.
Title   Home Telephone Number

_____   ____ / ____ _____
Spouse Name (Last, First, Middle)   Spouse Date of Birth   Spouse Social Security Number*

➢ _____   ____ / ____ _____ _____
Name (Last, First, Middle)   Date of Birth   Social Security Number*   % Owned

_____   _____
Home Address (Street or PO Box)   City   State   Zip code

_____   Are you married? ☐ Yes ☐ No If yes, enter spouse information below.
Title   Home Telephone Number

_____   ____ / ____ _____
Spouse Name (Last, First, Middle)   Spouse Date of Birth   Spouse Social Security Number*

➢ _____   ____ / ____ _____ _____
Name (Last, First, Middle)   Date of Birth   Social Security Number*   % Owned

_____   _____
Home Address (Street or PO Box)   City   State   Zip code

_____   Are you married? ☐ Yes ☐ No If yes, enter spouse information below.
Title   Home Telephone Number

_____   ____ / ____ _____
Spouse Name (Last, First, Middle)   Spouse Date of Birth   Spouse Social Security Number*

*The Social Security Number is required for all sole proprietors. It is also required for all partners, officers, and LLC members of businesses that will have employees, and all owners and spouses of businesses that will have liquor, lottery or private investigator licenses. Not fully completing section "f" will result in application delays. (RCW 26.23.150, RCW 50.12.070)

Chapter 5 – Sales Tax Compliance

Now that you have successfully registered your business with the state department of revenue, what next?

Obtaining a sales tax license exposes your business to several new requirements:

Collecting sales tax on taxable sales to your customers located in that state.

Timely filing a sales/use tax return based on the tax you collected from customers in that state. This can be monthly, quarterly, semi-annual, annual or in some rare cases, occasional. You probably noticed a question on the application asking something similar to "approximately how much sales tax do you estimate you will collect per month?" or "approximately how much taxable sales do you anticipate?" and followed by multiple answers which give dollar ranges. What the state is attempting to do is assign your business a filing frequency, meaning how often you are required to file a return. Generally speaking, if you plan to remit over $1,000 per quarter (3 month period) then you will probably be assigned a monthly frequency, meaning you will have to file every month.

Maintaining accurate books and records such as copies of invoices for your sales as well as purchases you may have made in that state. This is to protect you in case of questions by the department of revenue as well as in case of an audit, which I will discuss later.

Obtaining proper resale exemption certificate documentation, links to the forms are provided below as well.

If you are selling via Amazon's FBA program, they have offered as a service to your business and for a small fee, to collect sales tax on taxable items when each sale occurs where you have indicated you have nexus and obtained the proper licensing. Below I have provided links to the Amazon tax collection documents which I encourage readers to read and print (note this is directly from Amazon's website):

Tax Collection Service Terms –

http://www.amazon.com/gp/help/customer/display.html/ref=help_sea rch_1-1?ie=UTF8&nodeId=200787200

How Tax Collection Services Works –

http://www.amazon.com/gp/help/customer/display.html/ref=help_sea rch_1-2?ie=UTF8&nodeId=200787680

Product Tax Codes –

http://www.amazon.com/gp/help/customer/display.html/ref=help_sea rch_1-3?ie=UTF8&nodeId=200794480

Amazon has really simplified the process for online sellers who participate in their program, but there are a few important notes to discuss. Amazon product codes are pre-populated with a taxing decision based on canned taxability rules that are provided by their tax engine (Vertex). You will notice that Amazon leaves it to the retailer to confirm that the product code taxability is accurate based on what they are selling and where. Taxability decisions are state by state and as such it is difficult to include a tax matrix or taxability chart here in this chapter. As an example, clothing in the state of New Jersey is excluded from the definition of tangible personal property subject to tax, but clothing in New York is subject to New York sales and use tax. Secondly, while Amazon takes the tax collection responsibility for this service, they will not complete sales/use tax returns for the retailers and they will not remit the sales tax directly to the state department of revenue. Both of those responsibilities are still that of the online retailer.

Filing of sales/use tax returns can be somewhat of a burden to online retailers or small businesses which have not had such responsibility in the past. One thing that most individuals do not realize is that most taxing jurisdictions will compensate vendors for remitting sales tax to the department of revenue! That's right; you read that correctly, most states will compensate you for timely filing your sales and use tax returns!! The catch is that the amount which you can be compensated is generally anywhere from .10% to 2% of the tax you collect or intend to remit (also states on occasion change the percentage that vendors or retailers get to keep). So the more you remit each filing period, the more you get to keep. The compensation is typically noted as "vendor's compensation" or "dealer's discount". See line 9 of the Virginia Sales and Use Tax Return Form ST-9A:

http://www.tax.virginia.gov/taxforms/Business/Sales%20and%20Use%20Tax/ST-9,%20ST9A.pdf

In addition, more states are coming onboard with the concept of web-filing or e-filing of their returns such that a paper copy need not be filed (some states even require web filing for taxpayers that meet a threshold of $XX dollars per month).

An important note should be discussed here, when you register with a state for sales and use tax compliance and are issued a filing frequency the state department of revenue will expect a return on those dates. If a return is not received by the due date then a delinquency notice is usually auto-generated. This notice will generally read that your sales and use tax return was not timely received and should be filed immediately. If the due date on the initial notice is missed then often times the state department of revenue will estimate your tax liability (sometimes based on prior filed returns and sometimes simply pulled out of thin air) and assess your business for the estimated liability until the department of revenue receives the sales and use tax return in question with the actual tax due reported and paid. It is extremely important not to ignore sales and use tax notices received. These can turn into huge headaches and could even become valid and lead to tax liens or garnishments. If a sales and use tax notice is received you should immediately follow the directions on the notice to have the notices resolved. Often times there is a telephone number on the notice and I recommend calling the department of revenue and notify them that you are working on providing the requested information as soon as possible. Document who you spoke with, both name and number, and respond when you say you will.

TAXABILITY

As mentioned above, in most states, sales of tangible personal property at retail are generally considered taxable unless a specific exemption or exclusion applies. What this means is in most cases the sales are considered taxable. It would be difficult to list an all encompassing tax decision matrix here but I would like to point out a few of the areas which can and often do have different taxing decisions, depending on the state:

Clothing

Food or Grocery Items

Medicine

Medical Care Supplies

Questions regarding the taxability of specific tangible personal property should be directed to a qualified sales tax professional.

REFUNDS AND OVERPAYMENTS

Often times in retail transactions, sales tax may be collected in error. Generally there are several reasons for this but the most common reason is simple, a vendor or supplier makes a sale to a retailer who intends to resale the product but has failed to provide an acceptable resale certificate. The retailer who purchased the product with intent to resale is now in a situation where they are required to collect sales tax on the sale to the end user or ultimate consumer yet they paid tax to their supplier. The question now becomes, who is eligible for a refund of the sales tax paid in error? In simple terms, the answer is whoever paid the tax to the state department of revenue. But in this case didn't both the supplier and retail vendor pay tax to the department of revenue that they collected? The answer is yes, they both did. So, let's look at this a little closer and see which tax is legally due on the transaction.

Here is the example with hypothetical numbers to illustrate the point:

ABC Supplier Company sells to XYZ Retailer Company a book for $50.00 and collects 5.0% Kansas sales tax of $2.50 from XYZ and remits the tax to Kansas but XYZ failed to provide its KS resale exemption certificate.
Total Sale $52.50

XYZ Retailer Company marks up the book and sells it to Joe Schmo via Amazon for $75.00 plus the 5.0% Kansas sales tax of $3.75 and remits the tax to Kansas. Joe Schmo does not have any exemption certificate for the book.
Total Sale $78.75

Both ABC and XYZ were obligated to collect tax in lieu of an exemption certificate. In this case most states would direct the companies to do the following. XYZ should reach out to ABC and provide them their Kansas resale certificate and ask for a refund of the $2.50 in sales tax paid. ABC should refund XYZ the tax directly then request a refund of the tax from the Kansas department of revenue providing the resale certificate of XYZ as proof that the sale between ABC and XYZ should not have had sales tax applied. This scenario would "right the wrong" of XYZ failing to provide their Kansas resale exemption certificate at the time of the sale.

This is a very simplified example and often times there are "hiccups" in the process where vendors do not want to cooperate or forms and certificates are not completed, etc. However, there are additional remediation options to allow refunds or credits of the sales tax in question. Please contact a qualified sales tax professional to discuss fact specific situations and options.

The information presented in this chapter is not all-inclusive but should be used for information purposes only and as a guide to ask questions of your sales tax professional. The world of sales and use tax is often times confusing and slightly vague in nature. It does not have to be overly difficult to grasp once some basic knowledge is gained. Hopefully by reading this chapter it has triggered several questions you might have about your business as well as enlightened and helped clarify some of the more common and confusing sales and use tax issues.

Chapter 6 – Resale Exemptions

Most people mistakenly call particular transactions that are not necessarily subject to sales or use tax exempt in all situations. This is not necessarily the case. There are two concepts at play here, exemptions and exclusions. Exemptions are transactions which would otherwise be subject to sales and use tax if a valid exemption certificate is not presented at the time of the transaction. A common example of this is resale exemptions and this is why the states maintain resale exemption certificates. Exclusion is a transaction which was never intended to be taxed under the sales and use tax statute, therefore does not require an exemption certificate to be excluded from the tax base. A common example of this is legal or accounting services. Most states exclude these types of transactions from the tax base and therefore do not require an exemption certificate to be given / retained.

When sourcing products to sell online, whether it is from a wholesaler, retailer or some other supplier, a properly completed, valid resale exemption certificate should be presented at the time of purchase in order for your supplier to properly document the sale as sales tax exempt. If you are dealing with a wholesaler or the manufacturer of the product, they are generally quite familiar with this documentation and will probably ask you if you are sales tax exempt. This is the time to present the documentation. Conversely, when sourcing from a retailer at the point of sale (for example sourcing at Kohl's or Target), you could potentially run into a cashier or store manager who is unfamiliar with the concept of a resale transaction. Typically when they see tax-exempt customers, they are dealing with non-profits or some other specifically exempt individual or organization. As a retailer you are not specifically exempt similar to these organizations. You are only exempt to the extent you present a properly completed, valid resale certificate and it is quite possible the store manager or cashier is skeptical or denies the exemption out of sheer lack of knowledge. If this happens, there are ways to recover sales taxes paid in error. I will discuss this further in the chapter under Refund Requests. As a general rule it is easier to properly document the transaction as resale exempt at the time the transaction takes place as opposed to attempting to obtain a refund of sales taxes paid in error either from the state department of revenue or the vendor who sold you the product.

By now you may have seen the phrase "properly completed, valid resale exemption certificate" and think to yourself, "what is a properly completed, valid resale exemption certificate?" I am glad you asked because in order for the certificate to be accepted by both your supplier and the state department of revenue there are several elements which must be on the form or else either party (supplier or purchaser) can be held liable if the certificate is deemed by the department of revenue to be invalid.

These elements include but are not limited to:

- Name of the Purchaser (Your business name)
- Purchaser's address
- Name of the seller or supplier (who you are buying the product from)
- Seller's address
- Date of the sale or transaction
- State Tax ID number (the same number you were issued from the department of revenue)
- Description of the item(s) purchased
- Intended use of the products or items used
- Signature

Example: Indiana Resale Exemption Certificate ST-28a

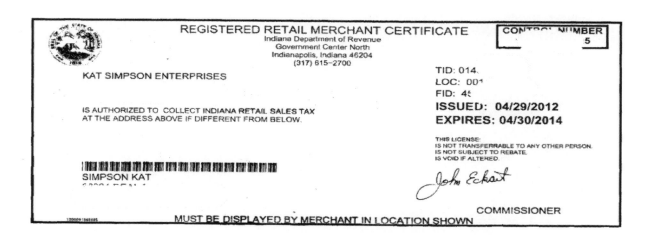

Chapter 7 – Audit Issues

Often times a new business which registers with a state department of revenue could be caught off guard when the state contacts the business owner or manager for a routine audit of their sales and use tax books / records. Every taxing jurisdiction that imposes a sales and use tax also has the authority to conduct audits and review the books and records of the businesses which are conducting business in their state. Often times the size of the business is not a factor in the decision by the department of revenue to conduct an audit, so it would be in the best interest of all taxpayers to prepare as if an audit could come at any time, meaning keep accurate sales records, copies of all sales invoices, all purchase invoices, copies of all sales and use tax returns (and checks used to pay the tax) filed as well as copies of all resale certificates. This is not a complete list but it is a start and the bulk of what an auditor might request to see.

The audit process generally (all states are different and this is a high level generalized version of what the process is) follows this process:

State determines which business it intends to audit based on sales tax registration or licensing rolls they have on file, documentation from other state agencies within the same state or documentation, or information gathered from other audits of taxpayers in the state.

Department of Revenue decides if the audit will be a desk audit or field audit (desk audit simply means they intend to complete the review without actually visiting your office which very well could be your home)

Department of revenue notifies the taxpayer of its intent to audit via a certified letter directing the taxpayer to call a specific auditor or to expect a call from a specific person.

Within the notification of audit, generally there is a list of all documentation they wish to review.

Department of revenue will schedule time to visit your office to review the documentation gathered at an agreed upon time.

Upon completion of the review by the department of revenue, if there is a liability discovered schedules of the adjustments will be provided to the taxpayer for review.

Generally the auditor will ask the taxpayer to review and agree to their findings. If an agreement cannot be reached, the taxpayer should be provided with a copy of the states audit appeals process and procedure guidelines.

At this point some states differ in that an audit supervisor could be called in to see if an agreement can be reached or the audit could be sent to an independent arbiter for a decision.

If all possible appeals / hearings processes have been exhausted, the final step is that either party could file a lawsuit in their respective district court for a judge to hear arguments and rule on the case.

A sales and use tax audit does not have to be an overly stressful or fearful situation but cooperation with the state representative is highly encouraged as they generally have latitude to waive or abate any potential interest or penalties which could be assessed on liabilities they find. If you are difficult to work with and non-responsive then they have no motivation to waive or abate any additional fees which might be assessed.

Chapter 8 – Setting Up Your Amazon Account For Sales Tax

Now that you have registered with the appropriate states and received your sales tax license(s) you will need to make sure that your Amazon Seller Account is set up to collect sales tax in those states, and also that your products are correctly marked as taxable. You can individually go through your inventory and mark each item as taxable using the Amazon tax code settings found under Settings: Tax Settings: View Master Product Tax Codes and Rules. Or you can mark all products with the default codes of: A_GEN_TAX (Always Taxable) and A_GEN_NOTAX (Always Nontaxable). You can set all products to the generic code on the same page you set up the sales tax collections, which is found from your Amazon Seller Central Home Page: Settings: Tax Settings: View/Edit Your Tax Collection Obligations and Shipping & Handling and Gift Wrap Tax Settings.

Here are a few screenshots from Amazon Seller Central to show you how to set up your Amazon inventory as taxable.

In the seller central main page under settings, you are looking for Tax Settings.

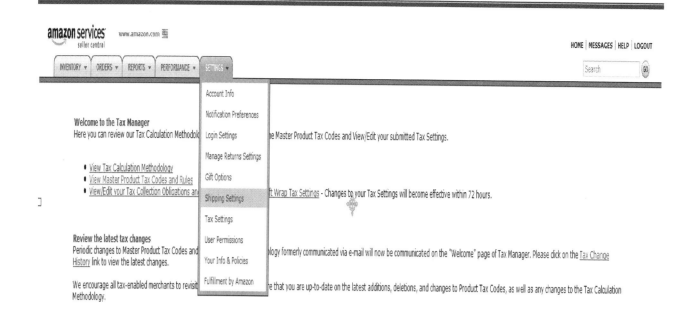

This is where you will land – and you can read all of this and then scroll down.

1. Choose your Product Tax Codes

You can make two levels of product tax code (PTC) assignments: seller-defined default assignments and offer level assignments. A seller-defined default assignment can be used to choose a single PTC that will apply to multiple offers. An offer level assignment applies on an individual offer basis and can also be used to choose a PTC for offers for which you wish to deviate from your seller-defined default PTC.

To assign a seller-defined default PTC, you need to both check the "Use default Product Tax Code" box and select the desired PTC from the drop down menu. To change a seller-defined default PTC you have previously assigned, select a new PTC from the drop down menu. To remove your seller-defined default PTC, uncheck the box. You can make an offer level PTC assignment through your listings feed or the Add a Product feature in Seller Central.

Note: For any offers to which you do not assign either a seller-defined default PTC or an offer level PTC, the Always Nontaxable PTC (A_GEN_NOTAX) will be used.

2. Specify your Tax Collection Obligations (States, Counties, Cities, Districts)

Indicate the tax jurisdiction levels for which you want the Tax Calculation Engine to calculate taxes and other transaction-based charges supported by our tax collection services. If you want to calculate taxes and other transaction-based charges at a particular tax jurisdiction level, click on the appropriate checkbox. Jurisdictions that you have previously enabled for our tax collection services have checks in their relevant checkboxes. If you do not want to calculate taxes or other transaction-based charges at a particular tax jurisdiction level, leave the checkbox blank, or if it is already checked, click the box to remove the check.

Example: By checking the California state and county boxes, you are instructing us to calculate California state and county taxes and other transaction-based charges when applicable in conjunction with other settings determined by you. With this configuration, you are instructing us not to calculate any California city and/or district taxes or transaction-based charges.

Note: For each state in which you have instructed us to collect any level of tax, you will need to input your state-issued registration number.

3. Specify a Custom Rate per State (Optional)

The custom rate feature allows you to enter a single override tax rate per state. If you enter a custom rate for a state, the custom rate will override the standard sales and use tax rates for all tax jurisdictions in that state (as supplied by our third party tax software provider).

Note: When you specify a custom rate override in a state, the custom rate (A_CUSTOM_RATE) will be used for all sales of products you ship to that state (regardless of whether you use seller-defined default PTC assignments or offer level PTC assignments), with the exception of offers to which the Always Nontaxable PTC (A_GEN_NOTAX) applies.

To specify a custom rate, check the "Use Custom Rate" box for the desired state, and enter a single override tax rate in the format we require. For example, if you want to collect 4.3750%, enter 4.3750 in the space provided next to the checked box for the state.

Please visit e-ComSalesTax.com for more information

This is where you will check to collect sales tax and select your 'jurisdictions' and also need to enter your Sales Tax License number from the states where you are registered. This is also where you can set your entire inventory to be taxable. Then at the bottom click Continue.

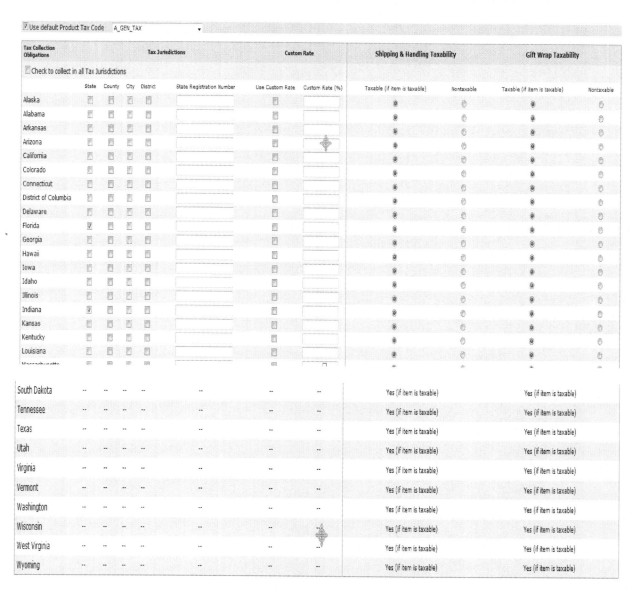

Next page is another confirmation page – be sure to click all three boxes.

Confirm Your Tax Collection Services Set Up

After you have (i) reviewed the tax calculation methodology and the product tax codes and associated rules, and (ii) set up and reviewed your tax collection settings, you may confirm your tax collection services set up. Use your browser's back button if you choose to look back at any of these steps.

Note: Taxes will not be collected for you until you have completed this confirmation. Your use of the tax collection services is subject to your seller agreement. Fees may apply to these services as described in your seller agreement.

☐ I have reviewed and accept the Tax Calculation Methodology
☐ I have reviewed and accept the Product Tax Codes
☐ I have reviewed and accept my Tax Collection Settings

Success Screen!

You have successfully completed your Tax Settings. Your Tax Settings will become effective within 72 hours.

Thanks for confirming your Tax Collection Settings Changes.

Return to Tax Manager

Chapter 9 – Finding My Numbers

Okay, you've signed up with the states, set up your account on Amazon to collect tax, NOW how do you find the amounts of sales you've had in these states so that you can pay your taxes?

There are reports in Seller Central that you can download to your computer, open in Microsoft Excel or another spreadsheet program and then sort them by the STATE column to find the orders you need to pay tax for. Then you will need to add up the totals of those orders for your sales tax forms.

I (Kat) have found an easier way to recommend. Outright.com is an online accounting system. They offer a free trial and their premium account is free right now. In Outright you can go into the reports feature and do a sales tax report. This report will give you all the totals for every state and make it very easy to fill in those state forms. Here is a screenshot of my Outright account for the first quarter of 2012. Notice not all states are listed, for those not listed I had no sales during the first quarter time period.

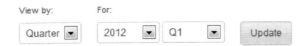

View by:	For:		
Quarter ▼	2012 ▼	Q1 ▼	Update

State	Number of Sales	Amount Collected
AK	3	$15.00
CA	8	$127.62
CO	2	$24.47
CT	4	$38.78
DE	2	$17.89
DKI JAKARTA	10	$124.57
FL	18	$209.25
GA	4	$156.49
IA	3	$44.35
IL	7	$84.38
IN	6	$83.69
KS	2	$10.65
KY	3	$91.56
LA	3	$77.65
MA	6	$100.55
MD	1	$44.90
MI	3	$29.55
NC	2	$18.94
NE	1	$15.00
NJ	2	$20.49
NV	1	$35.00
NY	6	$29.91

Chapter 10 – Conclusion

As mentioned earlier, this booklet was not intended to be an all encompassing sales and use tax answer source for every possible situation, but rather my vision was to answer some of the most frequently asked questions received from clients as well as provide some useful tips that I have picked up over the years in this industry. I wanted the focus of this book to be on the states which are most active with Amazon sellers, those being the states in which Amazon has a fulfillment center and as such Nexus tends to be a hot topic.

As a small to medium sized business owner, the burden of proof will ultimately fall on you, the taxpayer, to ensure compliance with the applicable sales and use tax laws and rules in the taxing jurisdictions in which you conduct business, but the concepts in this book can be applied to taxing jurisdictions not mentioned herein. Topics covered such as audits, compliance, reselling, etc. can be carried over to just about all-taxing jurisdictions. These topics are important regardless of your industry.

We live in a free market country which promotes innovation and allows for individuals to pursue businesses and opportunities which others do not have. To this end, there are still rules and regulations in place which we must follow, sales and use tax for retailers be it online or brick and mortar are just one of the many we must account for.

As I mentioned previously, don't see the obligation to collect sales or use tax as a hindrance to your business success. As your business grows there will be many other newly acquired functions (requirements) which involve time, effort and money to continue to be successful.

18040721R00052

Made in the USA
Lexington, KY
13 October 2012